To my two little girl friends!
"Corinne"

LITTLE TYKE

Little Tyke and her mistress, Margaret Westbeau.

The Amazing True Story of the
World-Famous
Vegetarian African Lioness

Little Tyke

by GEORGES H. WESTBEAU

Photographs by the Author

PACIFIC PRESS PUBLISHING ASSOCIATION

MOUNTAIN VIEW, CALIFORNIA

Omaha, Nebraska   Portland, Oregon

DEDICATED

TO MY WIFE, MARGARET

whose tender care and affection for our many creatures of the wild, which we gather around us at Hidden Valley Ranch, has helped to make possible this beautiful story, which is a reflection of her unselfish love.

CONTENTS

Raising a Lion Cub 1

Little Tyke and Pinky 13

Chased Away by Dogs 19

Becky 22

Kicked by a Horse 33

The Wreck 37

Sense of Liking or Disliking 40

Living Together 49

At the Zoo 56

Aboard Parade Float 62

First Snow 67

Earthquake 69

Pulling a Sled 75

Film of Little Tyke 78

Imp 85

A Host of Friends 89

Taking Motion Pictures 92

"Lion of My Dreams" 105

INTRODUCTION

Born to a bewildered and frustrated mother on a bleak September morning, Little Tyke set the world thinking anew. She was to fire the deepest thoughts within us and to remind us of Biblical prophecy. She was to bring out the heartfelt tenderness within us in a most unsuspecting manner.

As I write I think of the beautiful letters from thousands of wonderful people whom I have never had the pleasure of meeting personally. To one letter I give particular attention, for it reads in part: "I would advise you to stick strictly to the facts, for even then it will seem like a fairy tale."

THE AUTHOR.

Hidden Valley Ranch,
Auburn, Washington.

Splints and bandages for Little Tyke.

Raising a Lion Cub

❧❧❧

W E STOOD with taut hands clutching nervously at the huge iron bars of the escape cage as we realized our inability to cope with the vicious, raging beast that was pacing to and fro within. Her pain-ridden, amber eyes defied our presence at scarcely a yard's distance. With bared claws and glistening fangs she roared and flung herself at us and clawed at the bars which separated us from certain death. As the moments crept slowly by, I wondered why I had consented to analyze the behavior of this raging mass of defiant fury.

As the curator of the zoo and I stood anxiously waiting in the lion house, my momentary fears suddenly faded and I grew strong with sympathetic pity, for I realized that this frustrated and bewildered lioness had a definite plan for her babies, who were about to be born.

The plywood wall which we had hurriedly placed around her cage afforded privacy—not quite complete, and much too late. Yes, she had definite plans with which I almost agreed. She was planning to repeat what she had done in the past—as the little cubs were born she had crushed them in her powerful jaws, tossed them into the air, and thrust them against the heavy iron bars to fall in little crumpled and lifeless heaps.

This raging lioness, about to become a mother for the fifth time during the last seven years, fought frantically at the prison bars where she was caged so we human creatures could peer curiously at her from "a safe distance."

Apparently this mother felt no security behind those cold, iron bars. Human beings had placed her there. They had teased and tortured her, watching her agony, and they were as capable of destroying her.

Some had said she was a born killer, but I didn't think so, for I had seen mothers of the wild stand over their newborn dead and give that heart-rending, empty wail as though they tried to call their babies back to life. This mother may have had her "reasons" for destroying her babies. There might be a chance that her lion cubs had been born cripples; animals sometimes kill their cripples. I had to find out, and this was my chance. Suddenly there was a scramble, as a newborn cub was thrown toward me. With split-second timing I grabbed and stood with a new ward that was to change my life and teach me many things. The mother's quick and powerful jaws had left their mark on the cub, and its right front leg dangled helplessly. Many thoughts

A hungry orphan cub finds a friend.

flooded my mind as I held the tiny cub close to my cheek, but all I could say was, "You poor little tyke."

Being thrust into the role of sole benefactor to the offspring of this raging lioness had been farthest from my mind when I had consented to make a study of the expectant mother. My only recompense was to be the satisfaction of pouring out upon this wounded cub my inexplicable love for animals. This love had been a part of me for as long as I can remember.

In fact, the first reprimand I received as a child came as the result of such a love. I was about four years old. I can remember that it was an autumn day when I followed a crippled squirrel deep into the forest, hoping it would let me bandage its injured leg. When darkness overtook me, I curled up in a beautiful bed of colorful dry leaves and, flanked by a huge, friendly cedar log, fell asleep. At dawn the next morning, I became slightly panic-stricken, for I realized I was lost and hungry. In the forests lived my friends, but there were also dangerous creatures—bears and cougers.

I eventually found my way home to the cabin where I lived with my pioneer parents, together with ten brothers and sisters. I shall never forget the warm friendliness of the old wood-burning cookstove in the kitchen. The crackle of the burning wood echoed throughout the cabin as I crawled behind it and fell into an exhausted sleep. I was too tired to ask why the cabin was deserted. But I was to find that the rest of the household were combing every inch of the forest for some trace of me.

That was the reason why there was no one to greet me but the friendly, warm cookstove.

This was a day many years later, when I drove home with the torn and bleeding "little tyke." The brisk winds were scattering the clouds and whisking multi-colored leaves from the branches. Some floated lazily on the emerald waters of beautiful Green River as it slowly wended its way to the sea. For more than two miles the river's sparkling waters flow through Hidden Valley Ranch. They were calm and unperturbed, but I was excited and expectant as I handed a three-pound bundle of soft, downy fur to my wife, Margaret. Curious peacocks lined the housetop, while our kittens peered through the white picket fence. Our two terrier dogs danced happily about us as my wife fondled the helpless little creature. But to those new, blurry eyes, seeing daylight for the first time, this was a big world, and—well, her greatest concern was a bottle of warm milk.

From the first, Little Tyke, the lion cub, was to learn freedom without fear, and love was to be her guiding light. Here she was to meet, and be a part of, the various animals of Hidden Valley Ranch. Here she was to grow up to be healthy and strong.

After careful examination, veterinarians suggested that we amputate the injured leg. We learned that the gland which lubricates the elbow joint had been ruptured by the mother's cruel fangs and that this fluid seemed to cause the skin and flesh of the foreleg to slough away. We placed Little Tyke's leg in splints, swathed the wound with modern miracle drugs, and bandaged it as firmly as possible. But to this little foundling, born into this world with two strikes against her, life was cruel; and she tried her best with her tiny teeth and claws to free the damaged leg.

Then my wife came up with an ingenious idea. She patterned a vest with one sleeve for this tiny cub. This she cut and sewed from fresh, clean linen, and we slipped the injured and bandaged leg into the sleeve. It worked, but after two days the draining wound saturated the bandages and vest. We carefully applied new medicine, bandages, splints and vests, but these frequent experiences became excruciating ordeals for the helpless little cub. I realized she would soon learn to associate us with this terrible pain and in turn it would certainly have a tendency to make her vicious as she grew older. Something had to be done; some psychology had to be applied. This paramount question rose before me as I slept fitfully between the three-hour feeding periods at night. Then an idea came to me. I had previously noticed an old woolen bathrobe of mine hanging in the basement. I retrieved the old bathrobe and we were ready for a new approach.

My wife and I had become very dexterous with the repeated tasks before us. Pads of gauze were cut to the right size and miracle drugs applied to the leg. Strips of adhesive tape were torn and the ends stuck to a handy rack above the dressing table. Everything that might facilitate matters was prepared in advance in order to shorten the painful operation. Then with a quiet swish I flung the old bathrobe over the sleeping cub and gently rolled her into it. I pulled the injured leg through one of the moth holes in the bathrobe while Margaret firmly held both ends of the fighting and squirming little bundle. With surgical shears I ripped the old dressings off and quickly applied the new. We never spoke during the dressings, but immediately after the last bandage was taped into place, we began calling, "Where's the little tyke? Where's Little Tyke?" while we unrolled her and made the "rescue." We were both eager to see the results of our new technique. Margaret and I stood in silent thanks as the little cub licked our hands in appreciation for the "rescue." The previous resentment in her pain-ridden eyes was missing, and we realized our plan had worked.

Days passed quickly, and twenty-four hours did not seem long enough for all the work that had to be done. There were cattle, horses, peacocks, chickens, and many other birds and animals to be cared for. Unfortunately the revenue from our animals was not great enough to pay for hired hands. In fact, the ranch did not pay. However, we had a small business in the little town, but that, too, was not big enough to pay for extra help. It took much hard work every weekday from nine in the morning until six at night, along with waiting on many customers; so, needless to say, we were two very tired people each night as we closed our doors.

We were fortunate in that we had living quarters at

Peaceful days at Hidden Valley Ranch.

the rear of the business, and all our weekday meals were prepared and eaten there, as well as the daytime meals for Little Tyke. While we were out in the front part of the store, we left the radio playing softly for her, and I think that is how she acquired her love for music.

After our business hours we had many chores at the ranch. Dressed in a little red sweater to keep her warm and to protect her injured leg, the little cub was carried with us constantly. During pleasant days we placed her on the soft grass as we worked, but soon we heard a pitiful whine and whimper. She had learned that with an, "Okay, Little Tyke!" we would whisk her up into our arms again, perhaps to a bottle of delicious, warm milk.

We learned, through constant study, that in the animal kingdom the mother usually has a solution for all problems. We learned, for instance, that in a case of constipation in lion cubs, the mother gently licks their little bottoms until the desired results are obtained. When we were confronted with this problem because of the cub's inactivity, I used a bit of soft tissue dipped in tepid water, and this helped me regulate Little Tyke's system, with the result that she never had a messy bed. With the application of sulfa drugs and antibiotics the leg began to heal, and the cub was on the road to health.

Then tragedy struck, and my wife was rushed to a hospital in the city for a major operation. Now there were more problems. With so many creatures depending entirely upon me and with a business in which a new employee could not be trained in less than three weeks, I undertook the task alone. My day began at five in the morning with chores of feeding and caring for our numerous animals and birds. At seven o'clock I drove to the hospital in the city to see my wife. Then I hurried back in order to open our place of business at nine. This business was a cold-storage plant, and customers and their problems came first. Whenever the telephone rang during the day, it startled me terribly, for I feared it might be bad news from the hospital. Then at six o'clock I closed the doors of the plant; repeated the chores at the ranch, and again raced more than twenty miles to the hospital.

During all this rushing excitement the little lion cub slept and ate regularly until I left her in the car while I visited Margaret. Being left alone, she began whimpering and crying. My wife was worse and needed a blood

transfusion, so of course I immediately presented myself as a donor. I had given blood many times hereto-
fore, but during all this hurry and anxiety I had forgotten that I had eaten a sketchy breakfast. After the
ordeal of a "slippery" vein, which had to be probed for
several times, I gave the pint of blood. The nurse told
me to lie quietly for about twenty minutes. Twenty
minutes to me was an eternity, with all that had to be
done, so as soon as the nurse left the room I tried to slip
quietly out and on my way. It didn't work, however,
and I slumped into a helpless heap on the floor. My
mind was clear, but my legs would not hold me up. The
cold-storage plant opened late that day, and Little Tyke
in the car had cried until she had gone into spasms.
Somehow I managed through the day, and that night I
fell into a tired sleep with the little cub in a basket at the
side of my bed. I didn't need an alarm clock, for every
three hours her lusty voice told me she was hungry.

During my next visit to the hospital I left the cub
with the veterinarian's wife, but that didn't work too
well either, because Little Tyke had become accustomed
to my voice. When she didn't hear me she began crying
frantically and would not eat. Something had to be
done. My wife was getting better, and I could think
more clearly now; so I purchased a little kit resembling
a doctor's bag, and lined it with several paper diapers.
I placed the cub snugly in it. When I reached the hospital, I rushed in the door and up the stairs to my wife's
room. I opened the bag, picked up the cub and a bottle

of warm milk which I had prepared, and fed Little Tyke. This went along smoothly for a few days until one morning at Margaret's bedside I was caught off guard by the nurse, who had slipped in so quietly I had not heard her. I will never forget my surprise as she inquired, "What have you got there?" I looked up from the chair where I sat holding the nursing cub, and replied quietly, "It's a little lion cub."

I expected to be thrown out right then and there, but the startled nurse began to smile. Sometimes a smile can mean so much. The word spread like wildfire; and for the next half hour the patients in the other rooms on that floor received less attention than usual. The nurses were in my wife's room, watching and patting the nursing cub. Then, someone shouted, "Jiggers! Here comes the superintendent!" This, I felt certain, would be the proverbial "boot," as I tucked the still hungry cub back into the bag.

But the news was out. It had spread through the hospital; and here stood the superintendent in the doorway. With her "What is this I hear?" I pulled Little Tyke out of the bag again and tried to regain my composure as she came over to the corner where I was standing, trying to get the cub to nurse on the bottle. To my astonishment, the superintendent smilingly took the cub from my hands and gave Little Tyke the bottle like a veteran. I sighed weakly and slumped into my chair.

From then on, the cub's regular visits were the hospital's special secret. After several weeks Margaret returned home, and more weeks went by until chores and business settled down to a normal routine once more— well, as normal as a topsy-turvy ranch could be, where tame raccoons played with a dozen varieties of pheasant, peafowl, and chickens; where even the deer and Canadian honker geese came up to the door for a handout. Even Petunia, the skunk, waddled up and waited patiently for her tidbit.

I tried to imagine Little Tyke's future as I visited the zoos and gazed upon these three- and four-hundred-pound monsters roaring their defiance to the world. I tried to imagine this little creature when she would be a full-grown lioness playing about the house with me. I'll have to admit that merely thinking about it left me worried at times. Then as I put the cub down onto the soft rug of our living room, I became panicky over the thought that she might not grow up at all because of those two big strikes against her.

She was now able to hold her head up from the rug for a few moments at a time, and she tried to make her way to me by pushing the splinted leg in front of her. She seemed very small and helpless as she struggled, and as I caught her up to my cheek, I heard myself saying, "So you're the 'king of beasts,' you Little Tyke!"

Bandages and dressings were now applied every other day, followed by the usual psychological "rescue" from the old moth-eaten bathrobe, and a bottle of warm milk.

Little Tyke and Pinky

✷✷ ✷✷ ✷✷

ABOUT three months before Little Tyke was born, our tabby cat had given birth to kittens in the attic of our old garage. When I climbed up to have a look at them, I noticed that one of the little fellows was completely hairless. I thought at first it was a pack rat, for pack rats are born without hair and their skin is a bright pink. But as this little fellow grew, he had beautiful long hair that was different in color from any I had ever seen—a light pink. As time went on he developed a beautiful white ruff around his neck. Very appropriately we named him Pinky. When we brought Little Tyke to Hidden Valley Ranch, Pinky took to her like a leech. Wherever we found Little Tyke, we also found Pinky—at play or asleep on top of a soft chair.

Every day when we drove to our plant, Little Tyke and Pinky went along. There they played together in the living quarters to the sound of soft radio music until they were tired and sleepy. They usually slept on the davenport, curled up together. Little Tyke's bottle of milk was an easy chore for us. We opened a can of evaporated milk and mixed it half and half with warm water from the faucet. Little Tyke soon learned to listen for the sound of running water when she was hungry.

When we arrived home at Hidden Valley Ranch in the evening, my first chore was to place Little Tyke and Pinky in the living room of the ranch house. Little Tyke always made straight for the fireplace, and every day she seemed just as surprised that the fire was not burning. She immediately began pacing up and down before the fireplace until I rolled in a huge alder log and started a blazing fire. Like a routine act in a play, she then dragged her little silk cushion close and dove into the middle of it. From there she would peer at me through large eyes—so large for such a little creature!—as if to say, "That's the way a well-trained master should act."

At three months the wound in Little Tyke's leg was definitely healing. She learned to romp and play as she favored the splinted leg. But here was another problem. Little Tyke was more than ten weeks old, and she should be starting on solid foods. We removed most of her rubber toys, leaving only her favorite doll, and replaced them with bones from a freshly-killed beef. One sniff of the bones was too much for Little Tyke. She immediately regurgitated all the food she held in her stomach. Later she learned to take some baby cereal mixed with her milk; but as we attempted to wean her and give her meat without success, we were alarmed as we thought of the reports of scientists who claimed that carnivorous animals, such as the lion, cannot live without meat. We set ourselves to the task of teaching Little Tyke to acquire an appetite for meat. Someone told us to mix fifteen drops of beef blood in her bottle of milk. We did, but she would not touch it. We tried ten drops, then five, and even one drop; but still Little Tyke would have no part of it. Someone else suggested that we mix hamburger and milk in the palm of one hand and plain milk in the other, then let her lap the milk first and swiftly change to the hand that held the milk and hamburger. I tried this, but Little Tyke turned away quickly, even though she was hungry. I wiped my hands on a nearby butcher's towel and picked the cub up in my arms, but the odor of the meat on my hands made her ill. She sensed the danger-smell of blood and hissed, with fear in her eyes, as she cringed in a corner of the davenport. I then washed my hands thoroughly, prepared a new bottle of milk, and picked up Little Tyke and her favorite doll. She nursed contentedly and went to sleep on her pillow with Pinky.

When Christmas Eve came, we had great plans for everyone, including Little Tyke. The family gathering was to be at my wife's folk's place in the city. That evening, while I worked out front, Margaret went back into the living quarters to take a shower, so we could leave for the festivities directly from the shop. We used a coal range for both cooking and heating. So after making a hot fire in the range, Margaret took her shower before feeding Little Tyke and Pinky. Little Tyke associated the running water with her feeding time; so when she heard the shower going she sat up and started toward the running water at the other end of the room. She would rather jump from one piece of furniture to another than walk on the floor. This time she jumped from the davenport, where she had been sleeping, to a low kitchen cupboard, and then directly upon the red-hot cookstove. There was a blood-curdling scream! I dashed in to find the little creature writhing on the floor in terrific pain. Margaret had reached the scene first and she had seen Little Tyke fall from the stove, where she had left the skin from all four pads of her feet and a strip from her tummy about four inches wide and six inches long.

We speeded all the medical aid possible, but needless to say, that Christmas was a sad one for us. Little Tyke, less than four months old, had had her second painful accident.

After the veterinarians had swathed her in medicated pads, we took her home to the ranch, where we lined a large paper carton with absorbent cotton for her bed. Pinky stuck by her side, licking and comforting her as best he knew how. When pain gave way to a few minutes of sleep, Pinky jumped out of the box to catch up on his sleep, but he remained close to the box. When Little Tyke awakened and began crying, Pinky jumped back to his pal and began his licking and soothing all over again. This routine was repeated about every fifteen minutes through the night.

All the animals at the Hidden Valley Ranch trusted Little Tyke.

Now the uphill grind to health began all over again. After approximately six weeks Little Tyke again took her first step on those sore feet. She had been thoroughly housebroken at two months, but lying helpless those long weeks without the use of her feet, she had to be trained all over again.

One evening we closed shop, drove home to Hidden Valley Ranch to do the chores, and when we went out for a drive, for some reason we did not take Pinky along, even though he loved to ride in the car with us. That was the last time we saw Pinky. Everyone wanted this unusual cat, and apparently some folks took him from the ranch that evening while we were away. I believe they would have brought him back to Little Tyke if they could have seen her hunt and cry for him. During the ensuing months she mourned the loss of her pal, eating little food and losing weight. She became so weak and thin, we were afraid she would die. She didn't want the company of other cats, she wanted only Pinky. Whenever a new cat came across her path, she always showed keen interest and hurriedly approached to smell it; but when it wasn't Pinky, she always turned away with the same mournful look.

After nine long months we removed the last splint and bandage. At first Little Tyke seemed to lack the courage to put her full weight of sixty-five pounds on the unsupported leg, but she soon learned to romp and play with the other animals at the ranch.

Chased Away By Dogs

❧❧❧

AS Little Tyke learned to rely on that healed leg, she wandered away from the house a little farther each day in her explorations of Hidden Valley Ranch. It was on one of these forays that a band of mischievous dogs slipped by us unnoticed and Little Tyke did not return at her regular feeding time.

We combed the wooded hillsides and scanned the riverbanks, but there wasn't a fresh track to give us a clue as to the direction she might have taken. Darkness overtook us, yet there was no familiar deep, growling meow in answer to our frantic calls. We telephoned all the radio stations in the nearby cities, telling them of our missing lion cub. (I must add here that their co-operation was wonderful.) They broadcast pleas that if anyone saw the lion cub, "Please don't shoot her." They went on to explain that she was tame and harmless, and that she loved to ride in cars. Their repeated broadcasts also advised listeners how to feed her and whom to notify if she were found. At dawn we were still scouring every inch of the territory where we felt she might have wandered. Soon neighbors joined in the hunt, and as more and more kindly folk became interested, word of seeing some unusual-looking animal came from all corners of two counties. We investigated every clue within miles, and the distant ones were left to friends.

The second day passed with no results, then the third. When night again enveloped the countryside I feared the worst had happened. Either one of the several packs of hunting hounds in the country had run her down and killed her, or some frantic person had destroyed her. Lions cannot climb trees or swim, and they do not have a great lung capacity for long-distance running. Therefore they are vulnerable to packs of hunting hounds. We weighed the idea that the frightened cub, if still alive, might hide when searching strangers approached, so with heavy hearts we thanked each one as we asked them to give up. A great many willing Boy Scouts had joined the hunt, and with a small reward they, also, were sent to their homes.

On the fourth day I joined my wife, who had managed to run the plant alone while I had directed the hunt. Darkness came early these winter days, and the nights were long. I had left the plant before sundown to do the chores before dark; and as I was about ready to return to the plant I heard a familiar and plaintive growl. It came from the direction of our elevated pool at the bottom of the hill opposite our ranch house where a rippling spring gave unlimited waters to hundreds of goldfish. I was almost afraid to look, but as I turned, I saw the leaves of the Philippine bamboo move and part. I leaped with joy as the gaunt cub swayed and dragged herself toward me. She was too weak to call. The emptiness and sorrow which had hung so heavily over Hidden Valley Ranch suddenly lifted as the glad word of Little Tyke's return spread like wildfire. "Little Tyke is home safe!"

She had lost approximately ten of her seventy pounds. For days, as we cuddled her close, she seemed to want to tell us something; but we, the human creatures who boast of our mental powers, could not understand the simple expressions of this creature of the wild. She probably had a story of her nightmarish wanderings and struggle against fatigue and hunger through those long days and bitter nights. To this day we have not learned where she went or where she hid.

Becky

❧❧❧

A T Hidden Valley Ranch our strange family continued to grow. Even a bristling porcupine,
which had been stranded high in an apple tree
in the middle of the nearby village, was brought here to
live in peace. Somehow I had managed to father a state
law which created more than four thousand acres into a
refuge where no firearms were allowed. Here I was later
to see beautiful Chinese pheasants seeking refuge from
the Nimrods' guns. Some of the birds were badly
wounded, and deer, some with pitifully mangled bones
or other gunshot wounds, came here to get well or to
die in peace.

We were happy with our work and with our various
wards. Even a crippled cygnet, a young black swan
from far-off Australia, came to live with us under the
protecting eye of Little Tyke. Then there was Racci, the
raccoon, who loved to tease and roll with Little Tyke.
He would sometimes climb a tree where he could sit and
call down, as only a coon can do. To the visitor, it was a

Lunch for two friends.

strange sight indeed to walk along the wooded trails by
the riverbanks with our unusual companions. Little
Tyke was always directly behind or beside us, then came
our two little terrier dogs and Racci, scampering along
the banks of the river and going for an occasional swim.
There was Baby, the white-tail deer, who strode so
proudly yet daintily as she followed this strange group.
And Becky, the lamb, who seemed to imagine they were
all from the same family. I presume she was right, too,
because originally they all came from the same Giver
of life.

Where did Becky come from? It was spring and lambing time, and I picked her up in a slaughterhouse. I went to see the man who tends the animals that were about to be slaughtered and asked him if he happened to have a newborn lamb. He said if I could wait until he drove a penful of cattle into the killing chute, he would look. I waited while he opened a huge gate and snapped his whip at the cattle. As I watched the animals, about a hundred in number being driven to slaughter, I noticed a cow in the middle of the herd circling and bawling nervously. The attendant was cursing madly because she was holding the rest of the herd back. As I watched, I shouted to him and said he would never get her out that way, because she had just given birth to a calf and was circling it with all her life to protect her new baby. When the attendant saw the calf he cursed and murmured something about a law where they would now be forced to keep and feed the cow for another thirty days. I gathered from his terse explanation that had the cow been butchered one minute before the calf was born, that would have been legal.

We then went back to the sheep corral, where I saw a beautiful white lamb only a few days old. I bought it immediately, then asked the man what he would have done with the lamb if I had not purchased it. "Oh, thrown it into the tankage pot, probably," was his only comment, as I bundled the soft little creature in my arms and turned away.

As I search through my Bible today, I find the commandment, "Thou shalt not kill." I can find nowhere that it means only human beings. I further find that in the beginning the law was given man that plainly states, "God said, Behold, I have given you every herb bearing seed, which is upon the face of all the earth, and every tree, in the which is the fruit of a tree yielding seed; to you it shall be for meat." Genesis 1:29.

One bright spring day, Margaret and I walked to a beautiful meadow where the animals always came up to visit with us. Here we introduced Becky, the lamb. She was something new, and the other creatures were very curious. The mares and their colts came close to smell, and then they continued their contented grazing. Bonnie, the burro, however, was the jealous one, and she didn't know whether she liked the lamb or not. Little Tyke lay among the group of animals and watched in silence.

At our cold-storage plant the visitors grew in number each day, as more and more people heard of the lioness who refused to eat meat. To us this was just one more problem. We enjoyed the visitors, but time became the paramount factor. To make this extra work worth while, Margaret suggested that we place a jar on the counter with a card reading, "We are glad to show you Little Tyke. In appreciation, will you please donate a coin to the Seattle Children's Orthopedic Hospital." When the first jar was full, we drove to the hospital. This was a field day for the kiddies and Little Tyke. Children came on crutches and canes, in wheel chairs and on litters, to the lawn where the lioness was playing. Reporters and photographers were present, and soon pictures appeared in the Sunday edition of one of the newspapers.

Then came hordes of visitors. Sometimes when we arrived home at the ranch, there would be fifty or sixty persons who had taken over the lawns and were picnicking there until we arrived with Little Tyke. One of the greatest ads in the town was this Little Tyke. Soon three of the top-ranking town brass called upon us at the plant and notified us that there had been some grumbles. We would have to build a high wooden fence so Little Tyke would not create an attraction so great as to become dangerous, for, after all, she was a lioness, wasn't she? So at a great expense, I built an eight-foot high, solid board fence around the lot at the rear of our plant. Just as I was hanging the last hinge on the gates, an order came from the same source to tear the fence down. This didn't seem like good logic to me, so I flatly refused. It wasn't long until we were in the headlines regularly in our weekly paper. Some of the captions read like this: "Battle Lines Form Over Lioness's Fence;" "Owner Protests Action Against Lioness's Fence;" and many others, until they finally called it a "grudge fence." That did it. We met with the town council and proved that the fence was a legal fence, and the lioness was not a menace. The next caption read: "Town O.K.'s Lioness." However the village council passed an ordinance stating that any dangerous animal "must be caged" while within the town's

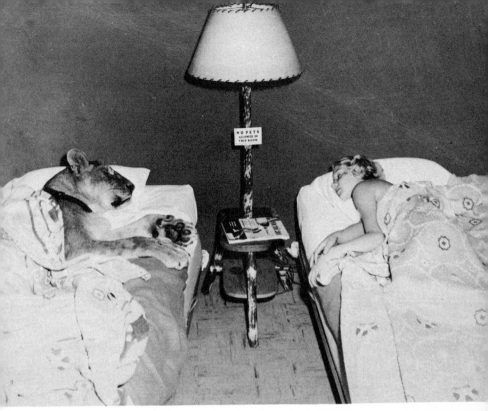

Little Tyke was a good guest, clean and neat.

limits. They sent us a copy of this law, and we knew it meant Little Tyke.

In the years that followed, Little Tyke brought thousands of visitors to the town. She appeared in practically every magazine and newspaper throughout the world, as well as in news-syndicate stories and over television. This publicity brought the little town to front-page news, yet this same village was the only town or city where Little Tyke was not allowed to walk down the street beside me. "A prophet is not without honor, but in his own country."

About this time we sold our cold-storage plant and moved to California. During her lifetime Little Tyke traveled more than one hundred thousand miles with us in our cars. When we stopped at motels we always got a large room with two double beds, one for Little Tyke and one for my wife and myself. We had learned that if Little Tyke was placed in a bed in another room, she worried all night, and every few minutes she got up and came into our room to see if we were still there. Wherever we went, she worried that we might leave her. She seemed to sense from the first that we were her sole benefactors, and that if we left her or she was lost, something would happen to her. Strangely enough, wherever we stopped we were always welcome to return with our unusual comrade.

At four years Little Tyke was a mature African lioness, and she weighed three hundred and fifty-two pounds. Every year she became more gentle. We had practically given up the hope of creating in Little Tyke a taste for meat. We advertised the fact that we were willing to pay one thousand dollars in cash to any person who could come up with a formula including meat that Little Tyke would eat, but nothing worked. We always questioned visitors who seemed to have more-than-average knowledge of animals if they knew of some formula containing meat which she would like, because scientists had repeatedly said that she could not live without meat. On one occasion I asked a young visitor this question, and it was he who put my mind at ease. He turned to

No, thanks! I'm a vegetarian.

look at me with serious eyes, then asked, "Don't you read your Bible?" I admitted I didn't read it as much as I probably should and then he continued, "Read Genesis 1:30, and you will get your answer." At my first opportunity I got my Bible and turned to the passage he had indicated. To my astonishment, I read these words: "And to every beast of the earth, and to every fowl of the air, and to everything that creepeth upon the earth, wherein there is life, I have given every green herb for meat: and it was so."

We didn't worry any more about Little Tyke's diet.

We had already worked out a diet which she loved. This diet consisted of cooked cereals, raw eggs, and milk. Did she thrive on it? Well, one of this country's most able zoo curators said Little Tyke was the best of her species he had ever viewed.

As the years went swiftly by, we learned of a new grain to add to Little Tyke's food. These numerous grains were carefully weighed, ground and mixed together while in their dry state so that they would form a sufficiently balanced diet of protein, carbohydrates, calcium, fats, and roughage. A few days' supply was always cooked in advance under Margaret's watchful eye and deft hands, and stored in the refrigerator until we portioned it out in Little Tyke's meals. She knew how much of this cooked grain to mix with the sweet milk, fresh eggs, and other ingredients which she added to make a nourishing and tasty meal. With a double handful of this cooked food, a half gallon of milk with two eggs mixed in it, Little Tyke was happy to crouch down and leisurely enjoy each meal. However, she refused to eat unless her favorite rubber doll sat beside her pan.

An occasional peafowl would stroll by to eye her luscious dish, but a deep growl would scare him away until her favorite peafowl appeared. Then Imp, the cat, would steal silently up to complete the strange group, and they settled down to dine. We fed Little Tyke in the morning and evening, and sometimes, when she became hungry, at midday.

To condition her teeth and gums we gave her heavy,

rubber boots in place of the bones which she had steadfastly refused to gnaw. One boot would last this strange
vegetarian from three weeks to a month. To start her
gnawing on a new one we always sprinkled it with sweet-
smelling perfume. To condition her stomach she would
spend an hour at a time eating the succulent tall grass in
the fields. When I look at the lions in the zoos, I wonder
if they, too, would not love to eat in the fields. We made
it a practice never to ask Little Tyke to give up a play-
thing or a toy without a reason, and then it was usually
with a trade.

On one occasion, I remember a lady friend of the
family visited us one day and quietly slipped off a tight
shoe. Little Tyke was quick to notice this, and with a
pounce she grabbed it and bounded away. I think she
knew she would gain our attention and that she would
be given a toy in exchange for her loot. I remember, too,
the day the heating oil man had playfully tossed her his
cap, and how like a frolicking puppy she repeatedly
teased him, almost allowing him to retrieve it, but sending him on his way without the hat.

There were many humorous moments intermingled
with the more serious. On one occasion we stopped at
a service station in Los Angeles, where one man serves
you with gasoline, another checks the oil, another checks
the air in your tires, while still another washes the wind-
shield and windows in your car. I went to all the other
fellows, winked slyly and told them to watch the man
who washed the windows. No one had seen Little Tyke

lying down inside our car. I jingled some money in my pocket and asked the fellow if he would wash the windows on the inside. With a "Yes, sir!" he opened the door. Then came a blood-curdling scream as he disappeared. Twenty minutes later, as I drove off, I saw him peering from behind a distant warehouse.

On another occasion, when a steel-plant executive visited our home, I left unexpectedly before dinner, stating that an emergency existed—a circus train had had an accident and some of the animals were loose. He remained to eat with the family, and I promised to return as soon as possible. The unsuspecting visitor didn't realize that we owned Little Tyke. While the visitor and Margaret were talking about where these wild animals on-the-loose might roam, Little Tyke pushed the door open and headed straight for the wilting visitor. He was a pretty good sport, however, and after a two-hour respite, he was able to continue his dinner!

Kicked By a Horse

❧❧❧

WHILE walking through the meadows with Little Tyke one bright spring morning, we came upon the horses galloping about and kicking their heels high as though they were especially glad to see the first shafts of sunshine gleam down through the huge, friendly maple trees. One three-year-old stallion, who seemed to be especially enjoying the frolic, reared to paw the air, and again stamped the earth to fling his heels high. I hadn't noticed that Little Tyke had joined the play until I saw the playful stallion's hoof strike Little Tyke with a sickening thud, squarely in the lower jaw. She dropped like a felled ox, as though her life was coming to an end. Blood gushed from her mouth as I rushed to her side to make a quick diagnosis of the extent of her injury. Some teeth had been loosened, but her jaw was not broken. Most of the bleeding was from her lacerated tongue.

From the nearby stream I drew cool water with which to rinse and soothe the bleeding mouth. As conscious-

ness crept back into the stunned brain of this limp creature, she began to lick her blood-spattered front paws.
The horses gathered around us to watch, as though they
were truly sorry. For a few minutes I worried, lest Little
Tyke might not be forgiving. However, my anxiety soon
vanished, and we began our slow journey back to the
ranch house.

For more than a week we fed the lioness liquid foods
and removed her rubber toys. Several weeks later we
noticed a soft pouch gathering under Little Tyke's jaw.
It seemed to contain a thin liquid. Margaret and I inspected it closely, then decided to take Little Tyke to the
nearby veterinarian. The doctor came out to our car,
where he stroked Little Tyke gently, as he had done
many times in the past, while he inspected the old injury.
She rolled playfully when he felt the apparently painless
sac. With an "I'll fix that!" the veterinarian disappeared
into the hospital. He emerged with a small surgical
lancet well hidden from Little Tyke's sight. As he
reached the car, Little Tyke's ears flattened to her head
and she snarled and with a warning growl rolled her
head from side to side. I called to the veterinarian and
cautioned him not to approach the car. I glanced back
at Little Tyke and saw that the pupils of her eyes had
narrowed to pinpoints. This, I knew, meant she was
serious. Only after the doctor had retreated into the hospital to dispose of the lancet, did Little Tyke allow him
to stroke her again. The intelligent doctor was quick to
realize the superior intuitive instincts of this creature.

Margaret, Georges and Little Tyke.

Many weeks later we visited the veterinarian of a large city zoo, and asked him to inspect the watery sac still clinging stubbornly to Little Tyke's jaw. We related our experiences with our local veterinarian. With a friendly monkey clinging tightly to one arm, the veterinarian stroked Little Tyke's head while he fingered the limp sac. I was astonished as this doctor warned me that the salivary gland had been ruptured, and that the sac was nature's way of stopping the flow of saliva until the gland could heal.

"If," he continued, "you had allowed the sac to be

lanced, the flowing saliva would have prevented the gland from healing properly, and would have dripped and dripped until it became necessary to operate and destroy the entire gland as far back as the brain. She apparently knew what was best for her." He smiled as he caressed Little Tyke.

It has been gratifying and reassuring to us to know that Little Tyke on no occasion desired revenge for the many hurts she suffered, and she continued to be friendly with all the animals of Hidden Valley Ranch.

The Wreck

❧❧❧

A T THE ranch there were many exciting adventures. Among these the breeding and caring for our many horses was by no means the least. Here we had Kentucky thoroughbreds, Arabs, and a few beautiful palomino riding horses. It was on such an occasion that I was to learn much of the memory of a lion.

I was returning to the ranch from a long and fatiguing drive with one of my mares and her colt in the trailer and Little Tyke perched royally on the rear seat of my car, when I was suddenly forced from the highway by a speeding car rounding the curve in my direction, on my side of the dividing line. I swerved off the pavement as the wild-eyed driver of the other car swished by, but as I tried to cut back on the highway again, my horse trailer skidded wildly; it struck a utility pole, which crushed the trailer hitch to splinters and sent the trailer, mare, and two-week-old colt catapulting crazily down the hill to the valley below. The force of the skidding trailer swung the car into the opposite direction, crashing

(37)

it directly into the steep bank of the hill. With a sickening thud the doors flew open, while the fenders wrinkled
and drooped like the ears of a tired hound. I managed
to back the car from the highway and got out to survey
the damage. Bits of the trailer lay strewn from the highway to the valley below; but somehow, in some miracu-
lous way, the mare and the colt had escaped harm. I
breathed a sigh of relief as I looked down upon the in-
different mare as she grazed contentedly in a pasture
while her spraddle-legged colt nursed.

Little Tyke was missing from her perch on the rear
seat and was nowhere to be seen. Fear grew within me
that she might be seriously injured and had crawled
away to die. I searched the hillside below for a hundred
yards in each direction, with no results. Then as cars
with curious people began to gather, I hurriedly crossed
the highway and ran up the hill. It was here, after what
seemed an eternity, that I found Little Tyke lying wide-
eyed with excitement under the low, friendly limbs of a
huge Douglas fir. As I approached she snarled viciously
and lashed out at me with a lightning paw. I sank to the
ground with a heavy heart as I fought off the fears which
crept into my mind. Would the result of this wreck in-
still the fear of the wild into the gentle and mild heart?
Could the fruits of our two and one-half years of loving
care be instantly changed into a mass of spitting fury?
Cynical prognosticators had forecast that someday she
would turn on me, but I still could not lose my confidence.

As the day faded into night I finally coaxed the frightened creature down the hill and into my car. She leaped quickly into the rear seat from where she had been flung, hissing, spitting, and lashing out at anything that moved about her. Night closed in around us as I hurriedly employed fence rails to bend fenders and tie rods back into shape. It was a long and tortuous way home through the dark, as the car limped and lurched at every turn. Those sharp claws lashed out at me with every turn and whenever I applied the brakes.

At home I didn't tell Margaret everything. I changed from the brown gabardine suit I had been wearing to khakis, which I usually wore at the ranch. Little Tyke seemed quite settled, so I prepared her food and put her to bed. Then I quickly readied one of the ranch trucks and went back to pick up the mare and the colt.

The next morning I was grateful to find that Little Tyke had regained her gentle disposition. I was not to learn until many weeks later that Little Tyke associated the accident with my brown gabardine suit. I later put on the suit, and she instantly snarled and struck at me in raging fury, so I gave up the idea of going anywhere with her that evening. When I changed back into khakis she immediately whimpered and eagerly nuzzled me. I understood now—it was the brown suit that had hurt both of us. Years later I donned that suit again, and once more Little Tyke was in a snarling fury. Needless to say, I didn't wear that suit threadbare; it had become a frightening reminder to the lioness.

Sense of Liking or Disliking

❧ ❧ ❧

LIKING or disliking people is instantaneous in most animals, yet I think this sense is amplified in the brain of a lion. I remember that when I walked down the streets, rushing to see Margaret in the hospital when Little Tyke was but a few days old, she would lash out at one passer-by and want to nuzzle another. Through all the years of her life she seemed to sense the innermost thoughts of people and if she disliked them she could stare them down or completely ignore them, as only a cat can do. Within seconds I could tell whether she was going to like a person or not. If she disliked him, the pupils of her eyes would narrow to pinpoints as she stiffened into that feline aloofness. On the other hand, if she liked the person, her eyes became soft and mellow as she rolled in the grass or licked his hands. When she met a gentleman she was quick to shake his hand; and when she met a lady she gently licked her hand. It was an occasion such as this that caused a feminine news commentator to veer from her strict and steadfast na-

Gloria Swanson and Tyke are friends at once.

tional news of state to say, "Last evening I walked across
the lawns of Hidden Valley Ranch with a full-grown
African lioness pressing at my side, and yet I was not
afraid!"

When Gloria Swanson visited the ranch for the first
time, she flung herself onto the lawn with Little Tyke as
though it had been a daily routine to caress the big cat.

Men and women from all walks of life and from
every corner of the earth somehow found their way to
Hidden Valley Ranch to see this unusual creature, and
though their first glimpse of this huge lioness sometimes
caused them to hesitate momentarily, it was a rare occasion that they did not reverently whisper, "And the lion
shall lie down with the lamb."

Asleep with a paw to the floor.

Little Tyke's greatest indoor pastime was to watch the wonders of television. From her selected place on the floor or on a davenport she watched intently her favorite "westerns." The galloping clatter of the horses' hoofs, or the sharp "bang" of the guns, increased her intense interest. When she grew tired she flattened herself at her full length of ten feet, four inches, and sank into a deep sleep, lulled by the soft music she loved so well.

Lions have a natural inclination to sleep with one front footpad flattened to the floor or ground where they lie. I believe this is because a delicate sense of feeling has been developed through the centuries until they have become uncanny in their sensitivity to vibration. Late in the evening, when Little Tyke had grown tired of watching her favorite television programs, she would amble over and nestle her huge head in Margaret's lap, begging to have her ears massaged. From this she would fall into a deep sleep until it was time to put her to bed for the night.

It was here that we learned of her marvelous sensitiveness. She would rise from one of those deep slumbers to sit up with tense alertness, then in a few seconds we could hear our watchful peafowl scream from their roosting places high in the treetops of the ranch. A few seconds later our dogs would bark as we heard a car approach the ranch driveway. Little Tyke was always the first to sense the approach of walking feet or the rolling crunch of automobile tires on the crushed gravel of our driveway. However, during late evenings we were always a bit puzzled over these warnings, which were generally from out of the unconsciousness of slumber.

When guests appeared, she would follow them from the opposite side of our long lilac hedge until they reached the gate. Here, if unnoticed, she would pounce out at them with breath-taking speed. Our "Keep Out" sign on the gate meant nothing to some people, and we soon learned to substitute alertness for those who would not read or heed. She taught many to believe in signs; but she loved the huge majority, even though to the stranger this was a frightening play.

From the time she was a tiny cub she loved to share our affections, and she constantly wandered from one to the other. Until she grew too large, she loved to lie with her hind quarters in one lap and her head in the other as we drove about in the car. If she had been following me about the ranch while Margaret was busy with her housework, she never forgot to amble into the house to spread herself full length on the kitchen floor to share her affection. I have seen Margaret go about her cooking or baking, stepping to and fro across this huge creature, who watched with keen interest, as though she was being taught her first lesson in the culinary art.

How accustomed can one become to having a lion in the house? Well, Margaret still laughs at me for my actions one day as I came in tired and hungry from working on the ranch, to slump into a soft, comfortable chair in the living room. I asked, "Where is Little Tyke?"

"Why, you just stepped over her when you came in through the door!" came her laughing reply.

I have heard Margaret say many times, "I would rather raise a dozen lions, if I had to raise them in the house, than to raise one dog." It is true that a lion will try to step in the driest and cleanest places before entering the house. There she will immediately set about cleaning and licking herself before lying down. A dog runs through the muddiest water and digs holes in the lawns and scratches up the flower beds to continue his coyotelike trot hour upon hour.

Little Tyke loved beauty; it was here in our flower gardens that she spent many early-morning hours stepping daintily from flower to flower, sniffing and drinking in the fragrance of each new bloom.

She loved to strike a pose for a picture with any of the countless number of visitors who came to see her. As the photo flash bulbs glared, her eyes danced in delight. It was because of this that we endearingly dubbed her "the ham."

As the eager visitor delved through the hundreds of pictures in our clubroom, it was her usual delight to press a huge paw on the latch of the door and make her way to a davenport by the fireplace where she listened as though she understood every spoken word.

As we traveled hither and yon with this huge lion sitting on the seat beside us, hanging shoulders and paws out of the window as we rode, we found it difficult to avoid the gathering of inquisitive crowds or to carry on the business for which we had come. I enjoyed showing her off as much as she enjoyed electrifying the wide-eyed crowds who instantly gathered around wherever we stopped. We purchased a sedan delivery, a sort of light panel body mounted on the light frame with springs of the sedan chassis and with one small window in the back. This afforded much privacy for Little Tyke, and allowed us to go on about our business as she slept. It was in this car that we visited a friend in the eastern part of the state. We decided to spend the night, and here, in her new car, Little Tyke learned that there was security from

ROG

Harold Russell enjoys a face washing.

prying eyes, and peaceful rest like that of her bed at home. We seldom cultivated the friendship of folk who did not like animals; so, needless to say, wherever we went, Little Tyke was as welcome as we were.

On this particular occasion, these friends lived in the country, and one extra bedroom was all they had. So very conveniently, when the evening grew late, we put Little Tyke to bed in the car on a thick, soft mattress. A few hours later, as one of the other guests left, I decided to take one last look at Little Tyke. With shocked surprise I noticed the rear door of the car was open and Little Tyke was nowhere in sight. I had failed to remove a very small catch on the inside of the door, and she had rubbed against it, unlatched the door and flung it wide open. My thoughts raced, for I remembered that within a hundred yards of the house were a busy highway and railroad tracks. With my flashlight in hand I ran into the night, calling, while the other visitor took "refuge" in the house. There was no familiar, grunting answer, and I did not hear her feline footsteps in the soft earth. I turned, and saw the barn door swing open. I hardly dared look, as I turned the light switch inside the doorway. With a sigh of relief I gazed upon that confident creature pacing back and forth behind a long row of horses and cattle like a general inspecting his guard. A bewildered hen flew, cackling crazily, from a pole on the manger, as I sat down to pat this grand creature who knew she had committed no wrong.

On our trip home the next day we laughed heartily

as we related the experiences I had on a similar trip with a friend before we purchased Little Tyke's car. This friend and I had started on the long trip with Little Tyke occupying the rear seat. After some hours Little Tyke decided she was lonely back there alone, and she proceeded to pour her three hundred fifty-two pounds between us in the front seat. My friend and I tipped the scales at more than two hundred pounds each, so needless to say, a few miles of the thusly-packed front seat was more than enough for my friend, especially with this happy and affectionate lioness turning and twisting to lick his sweating and anxious brow. He managed somehow to climb over and slide into the rear seat, and he smiled with well-earned satisfaction as he wiped her saliva from his cheek. His satisfaction was short-lived, however, for she yearned for his affection and forced him to clamber back and forth in numerous escapes as we drove that more than two hundred and fifty miles through the mountains.

Living Together

‰‰ ‰‰ ‰‰

W HILE at home or traveling about the country, Little Tyke always maintained her complete and implicit confidence in her mistress and me. If I found it necessary to scold her, she fled to Margaret to sob and cry; or, on the other hand, if my wife scolded her, Little Tyke came to me with her woes. To those who have never lived with a lion, it must be difficult to realize that these huge creatures can do anything but snarl, roar, and kill. But let me tell you with deep sincerity, that these much-maligned creatures have countless little sounds by which they make themselves understood to those who know them.

The animals of the wild I hold in highest esteem. They possess a seventh sense far beyond that of domestic animals and even that of man; and, contrary to the belief of many, they have no natural aversion to man. Through the centuries in which we have dominated the animals we now term "domestic," our dominating inhibitions have completely arrested their initiative until they have become dull beasts of burden or docile prisoners of our peculiar whims and desires. They have, in the main, lost the original intuitiveness of the creatures of the wild. We who boast of our mental prowess have steadfastly trod down that selfsame path until we have lost the intuitive ability man once possessed.

There is not an animal or bird who would not lovingly fraternize with man. You of the cities have but to go to your nearest lake to feed the ducks of the wild or to your wooded park to feed the gentle deer, to assure yourself of this truth.

But why are they wild and termed savage by man? Not because of their "bestial" desires, but because man has learned to maim and destroy, leaving these helpless creatures to be crowded into the forests and jungles for meager protection. There, in their shipwrecked state, without sufficient God-given food of the fields, they have learned to devour each other in their pitiful flight, just as man has repeatedly done and will do this day if circumstances bring him to a tragic plight without food.

If you were cornered by a madman who sought you out to satisfy his cruel and bloodthirsty lust, and you knew you were about to be killed without reason, would you not fight for your life? By your own reasoning, then, you would be called "savage." Animals of the wild are not savage; they are only scared of man and of what he has done to them.

Oh, the beautiful memories we possess of the times when we walked along the wooded banks of the river and through the flower-studded meadows with Little

Tyke! As I look back now I can understand how one of the nation's leading war correspondents, just back from the battle front, must have felt as he wrote about us: "He and his wife have tried to create a small world of their own where fear has no place, a tiny oasis of love, where the lamb and the lion can lie down in peace together. . . . Here the only discipline is that of love and freedom. And there is no reason to kill." Then, as though his fleeting thoughts rushed him back into the world of realities around us, he added, "However the experiment ends, they have created in Hidden Valley Ranch, for a short space in a troubled time, a two-hundred-acre world without war, hunger, or fear. And if it should turn out to be only a brief truce between all these lovely creatures and man, well, it is still worth remembering." What a diversion this must have been to him from the screaming shells overhead, the death-dealing blast of the bombs, and the pitiful call of the dying!

I also recall the time when we walked along the trails from meadow to meadow, as the gathering animals followed in our footsteps. There were anxious moments as we awaited word from our son. Then came the message that he was declared lost in the islands of the Pacific. It was hard for us, in our peaceful surroundings, to realize that the war-torn world and ours were on the same planet.

During our numerous trips to the beaches, I watched Little Tyke and her mistress play in the sands while the huge waves lapped to and fro. I watched them walk the

A peaceful rest by the Pacific Ocean.

smooth logs of driftwood. And as they walked upon the freshly-washed sands of the great Pacific Ocean, I thought: "What a fitting scene is this, for the name itself, Pacific, means 'peaceful.'"

In the southland she loved her early-morning walks through the sparsely growing sagebrush. It was here one day, when the sun first came up over the horizon, casting its long, silent shadows, that Little Tyke astounded me by bounding away, only to pounce upon me from her hiding place, which was usually a sagebrush. It was scarcely large enough to hide an animal the size of a house cat. As she dashed away again in her play, I tried to follow her or her shadow, with my eyes, but it was useless. To her delight, she always fooled me. In the midst of the desert we visited the date gardens. Here the close-growing trees provided a cool, green canopy where we could walk in the shade. The date harvest was in full swing, and the Mexicans used in this work were busily gathering the luscious fruit from their precariously high perches, while still others on the ground emptied the filled baskets into boxes and carried them off to the waiting trucks. We listened to their chanting songs as they worked, and then we continued our interesting journey. We didn't realize the odd scene we were creating until screams caused us to halt. All the workers vanished mysteriously within seconds, but as we listened, we could hear them chattering like magpies, high in the palms, looking at the strange sight below.

At a motel pool we swam and relaxed our pleasantly-tired bodies as we speculated on the next day's task. A producer of one of the larger motion picture studios in Hollywood had talked with us about the possibility of making a perilous desert scene with Little Tyke stalking a small child. This scene was to be the nucleus of a proposed motion picture. However, to the wary producer, this scene was a practical impossibility. "If Little Tyke will stalk and charge the child, will she stop without inflicting some harm?" he asked anxiously. And as though he thought the whole thing impossible, he added, "Supposing she will do all these fantastic things, what child could you find who would dare take the part?" Then, as if to cast the whole idea aside, he continued,

"And if you do find a small child who is willing and un-afraid, what hope is there of the parents' giving their consent?"

That evening we talked with a little girl and her parents about the possibility of obtaining the flaxen-haired child for the test shots. The girl had been afraid at first, but as she played with Little Tyke, she grew confident in the big cat's gentleness.

Early the next day we drove out to the drifting sands of the desert where the dunes blended beautifully with the bright morning sky. Here we set up our motion-picture equipment while the little girl and her parents played with Little Tyke. After a few brief moments of review, I walked out into the soft, shifting sands, where I commanded Little Tyke to lie down and remain still. Near the camera I placed the little girl, who I asked to take off her shoes and playfully cover her feet by sifting sand through her fingers. According to the script she was supposed to be out in the desert alone, and when she heard a distant growl she was to turn and look for a few moments and then resume her play. At the sound of the second, and louder growl, she was to pick up her shoes and start in the opposite direction, looking back over her shoulder with puzzled anxiety. Then when she heard Little Tyke roar she was to run for her life. I turned to her parents and warned them not to make a sound. I knew if they should scream, Little Tyke might not hear my commands, and might, from her confusion, fall too hard on the girl.

As I asked the girl to begin her play, I motioned to Little Tyke to crawl stalkingly low and to growl; then she crawled faster and faster until, with a roar, she realistically charged over the sands at the fleeing girl. Within seconds Little Tyke closed the distance between them, and with a last flying leap she sprang into the air, landing directly on the sprawling girl, enveloping them both in a huge cloud of dust. The next few minutes were like an eternity to the anxious parents as they waited for the dust to clear, but their confidence in us and in Little Tyke grew strong as they saw their prone child stir from under the huge body of the lioness standing over her. I was so intensely engrossed with the realistic action of this scene that I wonder now how I remembered to manipulate the camera. I saw the little girl extend a small arm to Little Tyke's neck as she pulled herself to her feet, then with a shake of her curly, tousled hair, she hugged the huge creature and caressingly remarked: "You stinker! You fell harder than you were supposed to!" She then placed her tiny hand on the lioness's neck and the two strolled over a distant sand dune as directed. I could hardly believe that the entire scene had been completed, and without retakes! At the studio projection room, where anxious producers and directors waited, I was pleased as these viewers could scarcely believe their eyes. To some this might have been a great risk; but with the confidence I had gained in living with this gentle creature for these many years, I knew exactly what Little Tyke would do.

At the Zoo

✕❦ ✕❦ ✕❦

ONE day the curator of the zoo where Little Tyke was born telephoned me to bring the lioness over to see whether she would recognize her parents. It was on a rainy weekday and we knew there wouldn't be many visitors at the zoo. We went directly to the lion house. Her mother and sire meant nothing to her, and she seemed to realize that there was no friendliness in them. Little Tyke walked to where a white cockatoo sat screeching in his raucous manner just outside the monkey cage. This seemed to annoy her, and she made straight for the exit door at the opposite end of the building. As I turned the knob, and she helped me open the door with her massive head, a woman was reaching for the doorknob from the outside, a few steps below. Little Tyke and this woman met nose to nose. With a terrified scream the lady turned and ran up the steep hill, while two men who were at the bottom of the steps, stood frozen in their tracks. At approximately a hundred yards' distance, the breathless woman paused for a quick glance to the rear. I knew from the expression on her face what she was thinking. She believed the lions had escaped and one was springing at her, making ready for a nice, fresh meal. Next came a look of consternation as she realized the lioness was not close upon her. I know I should not have laughed, but the tableau was so funny I couldn't help it. I sat down on the steps and petted Little Tyke and beckoned the woman to come back, indicating that Little Tyke was gentle. However, the woman waved me off and disappeared over the hill.

From the lion house we wandered across the lawn to the huge pool where the ducks, geese, and proud swans floated in splendor. Here Little Tyke lay down to watch with great interest, as she always did when she saw new creatures of the wild.

A little boy came running across the lawn, and to our amazement, he flung himself down before her. There he sat, oblivious of the others around him, staring into her eyes as though this had always been his secret trysting place with this huge and understanding creature. Those who had gathered around us stood in silence as they listened to the soft, eager voice of the boy chattering to Little Tyke, and she in turn listened as though she understood every word. I heard him say, "I'd rather have you than a dog!" Then as his excited words flew I heard him fervently repeat his love, "I'd rather have you than a *dozen* dogs!" Their noses were but inches apart, and this huge lioness seemed to have ears for no one but

"I'd rather have you than a million dogs!"

this eager lad. As we readied to leave I watched the little fellow fling his boyish arms around Little Tyke's neck, and, as though he had not fully impressed upon her his true love, he shouted to her with tear-dimmed eyes, "Little Tyke, I'd rather have you than a *million* dogs!" A parting picture which I took of them impressively graced the front page of that city's newspaper, and holds a favorite spot in our memories.

As we walked toward the park driveway where we had left Little Tyke's car, we found a traffic jam and a crowd of staring people. As we passed one of the cars, I heard a young lady exclaim, "Oh, how I would like to

have my picture taken with that beautiful lioness!" This
was an unusually delightful voice, so with a gesture and
a "Come on over and we'll do just that!" I stepped closer,
only to learn that this beautiful young lady was a helpless cripple. A deep tug at my heart prompted me to
open her car door and without hesitation I lifted her into
my arms and carried her onto the lawn where Little Tyke
lay. I shall never forget her radiant expression as she
caressingly buried her beautiful face in the silken hair
of Little Tyke's massive head.

Before entering Little Tyke's car we stopped momentarily at the cage where Butch, the big brown bear, was
housed. Butch raised up on his hind legs and pawed
through the bars toward Little Tyke while Little Tyke
looked longingly at him. As we bade good-by to the zoo,
the curator asked me if I would like another ward. A
doe in the deer pen had refused to care for her newborn
fawn. One look at the hungry, shivering creature and we
were overwhelmed with pity. We bundled the mass of
sprawling, spindly legs into our car and drove to Hidden
Valley Ranch, where our first chore was to prepare a
bottle of warm milk for our new foundling while Little
Tyke watched with keen delight. With plenty of nourishing food and constant care, which Margaret bestowed
upon all the creatures of Hidden Valley Ranch, the tiny
creature soon developed into a dainty and stately doe. Because she had had no mother to warn her of the dangers
of man and the forest, she soon learned to love us and
to mingle with the animals of Hidden Valley Ranch.

We named her "Baby" and it was with great delight that we watched this young deer play and walk with Little Tyke, Becky (who was now a full-grown sheep), and our numerous other wards. Baby was quick and proud as she strode daintily upon her slender legs to greet us and to give us a fond nuzzle on each cheek with her soft nose. I feel certain that if the State Game Department would allow any individual, who cared enough, to raise a pet fawn, there would be many, many thousands who would not want to shoot these gentle and harmless creatures or to cripple and maim countless others, who must crawl away to die in days of agony without any aid of anesthetics such as we humans have to allay our pain. Yes, we can be such sportsmen, when the innocent pay the agonizing bill!

Perhaps here I should give a kindly word of advice to the animal lovers who would like to raise a pet lion. (I never refer to Little Tyke as a pet, for here was a different and magnificently noble creature, a creature predestined to set man back on his haunches and make him think.) Don't raise a lion—ever! Man is a fearful animal, and the reaction of fear is savagery. These countless fears will be an obstacle in your path. As an example, I quote the following from a newspaper clipping: "Some time ago Kansas City witnessed one of the world's strangest executions—that of Zimba, a superb African lion. Zimba had grown up in the home of his owner— timid and gentle, he lived the life of a house cat, slept before the fire, ate only cooked meat. Eventually the powers that be forced the owner to send Zimba to the zoo. For a month the pet lion lay whimpering in the corner of his cage. He fled in terror when another lion approached, yet he begged for attention from any human being who passed. At last the owner decided that there was no place in the world for his beloved pet— who couldn't live with lions and wasn't permitted to live with men. So, over the protest of hundreds of persons, he ordered Zimba's execution. . . . Zimba played happily with his owner and the veterinarian. Quietly he entered the gas chamber. Then he went to sleep—killed by the only living creatures he did not fear."

Cruel experiences such as these, coupled with the thundering roar of fighter jets roaring overhead, jerks one into the reality that all is not peaceful in the world as it is here at Hidden Valley Ranch, where birds, like the animals, are free to roam, without the confinement of cages. The peacocks fly down from the surrounding trees at feeding time. In the spring they hatch their young on the wooded hillside, but always bring them home to our housing protection until they are able to fly and care for themselves. Peafowl seem to enjoy the whole day through, and so they never go to roost until the last shafts of sunshine have faded beyond the horizon.

Aboard Parade Float

IN THE springtime we are proud of our daffodil festival, which takes place in the neighboring cities, where more than fifty beautifully decorated floats take part. It was on one of these occasions that we were asked if Little Tyke might adorn a service-club float. This was a new venture, and I pondered over the idea. I decided to take the chance if I could use one of the heavier trucks of the ranch, in which she had ridden many times. The truck frame was rebuilt to suit the occasion, and thousands of daffodils were utilized in its decoration. At the rear top of this massive mound of flowers we built a throne of golden beauty. Here we placed a regal "queen," a little girl of eleven, with her color guard carrying spears, at each side. Two golden reins floated graciously forward from the hands of the "queen" to the gilded harness of Little Tyke. I would ride below. I had requested an escape hatch be cut overhead through which I might climb if something went wrong, or if any of the three small children became frightened atop this huge moving mass more than a dozen feet in the air.

We all climbed aboard to start the long trek of more than six hours through three cities. I sat on the hood of the truck, directly under the front of the float where Little Tyke stood. When I looked up I saw that the escape hatch was no more than a four-by-four-inch hole in the upper deck. I called to one of the workmen to hand me a carpenter's saw, and I hurriedly began the task of cutting an escape hatch large enough to allow all of my two hundred pounds to crawl through. To the keen eye, the tip of this saw could be seen furiously cutting its way as we rolled along the streets.

From little peepholes along the sides of the float I could see people staring as though they hardly dared entertain the thought that this real, live animal of the jungle was up there with those three small children. But to Little Tyke, the valiant trouper, this was a new experience. She loved the thunderous applause, intermingled with the soothing adjectives of endearment bestowed upon her.

Occasionally she would turn to vent a gaping yawn. Through the blinding sun that shown directly down into my eyes, I noticed Little Tyke wince; however, I paid no attention to it. The anxiety I had previously entertained had given way to proud satisfaction. Between cities we stopped long enough to give Little Tyke water and some cool milk, but it was not until we rolled along the streets of the last of the three cities that I noticed Little Tyke

Prize-winning float—a real lion for the Lions Club.

jump as though she suffered some severe and sudden pain. The next moment she tried desperately to crawl through the escape hatch, through which I had emerged, head and shoulders. But a few moments later we were at the end of the parade and I thrust myself up to the high deck where Little Tyke was lying. We hurried her down to her waiting car where she ate a well-earned meal. While she ate, I climbed atop the float to help the tired but smiling "queen" and her two little gallant guards descend. There I gathered a double handful of dried peas and beans from the spot where Little Tyke had been lying. With quick deduction, I realized that these were but a few of the missiles which had found their mark from the blowguns of youngsters. Later a witness told me of seeing a youngster shoot Little Tyke with an air rifle from his vantage point in a second-story window. I shuddered as I thought of what might have happened if Little Tyke had tried to jump from that high float. If she had been fortunate enough not to have broken a leg, someone surely would have become panic-stricken and destroyed her.

The following years brought many requests for Little Tyke to adorn floats, but with sickening thoughts of what might have happened during the one parade in which she participated, I smilingly declined. The first-place award she had won was not inducement enough for us to place Little Tyke's life at stake again.

However, many exciting and interesting experiences followed in the wake of that parade. We were invited to dine with the hosts of the service club, for whom she had just won first place—a prize they had never earned previously. Little Tyke and I walked down the busy streets of that city and entered the leading hotel, where a waiting elevator whisked us quickly to the tenth floor, there to pose with leading members for unique photographs. Here we were presented with a check for our labors, which I immediately endorsed and presented to the Children's Orthopedic Hospital Guild.

In the midst of this celebration we were called to nearby Fort Lewis, where Little Tyke joined in the dedi-

The first lioness to copilot a helicopter!

cation of its helicopter service. The skeptical pilot winced as he watched the lioness climb aboard and take her place in the copilot's seat. As cameras ground away, however, fear was cast to the four winds as the roaring blades carried the strange pair aloft. Airplanes, elevators, and helicopters were thrills to Little Tyke, as she recorded historical "firsts" in almost every such experience.

First Snow

ORIENTING the lion to the climate of the northern part of the country is routine in the zoos, but to try to orient the creature from the tropics to deep, drifted snow is another adventure. Little Tyke's first snow came when she was a fully matured lioness. I can almost see her now as she timidly came from her warm room to follow us about the ranch as we did the chores on this cold morning. She touched one large paw to the glistening white blanket which covered all the out-of-doors as far as she could see. She withdrew instantly, shook the flakes from her pads, and started to go back into the house. The temptation to follow us about as we worked was too great, however, so with one great leap, she piled out into it. We broke trail for a while, but soon she leaped and rolled about as though she had played in it for years.

Our horses and cattle seemed especially glad to see us, as they turned to follow in single file to the feeding sheds. Bonnie, the burro, was most jealous of our attentions; therefore she always led the herd, flinging her rear hoofs at the skies. She brayed and stamped in the newly fallen snow as if to ward off the affections of any of the other animals. Little Tyke lay down and sank deep into the snow at the edge of the trail, as she seemed to count off her friends one by one. Later, at the feeding sheds, she seemed thoroughly to enjoy the contented champing of the animals as she followed us along the mangers to find a vantage point atop the huge mound of hay.

Margaret suggested a walk in the crisp morning air. This was all it took to bring Little Tyke scampering down from the hay. We had long since learned it was necessary for us to spell the word "walk" if we were not in earnest. To her a broken promise was a sad disappointment, so away we went along the river and through the forest of snow-laden trees in this winter wonderland. We broke three distinct trails, as if we were exploring Hidden Valley Ranch for the first time. The thermometer hovered near the zero mark; the sound of the river ice crackled and echoed through the trees as we walked. At one point Little Tyke hesitated, glanced at the ice-laden waters, and shook a cold paw. At this intimation of chilliness on the part of the animal, we turned homeward. She was now content to romp ahead in the well-broken trails.

Earthquake

\/ \/ \/

I WAS busily at work in the ranch yard one day planting camellias, when I heard the screaming of peafowls. I looked up to see them flying crazily through the air, while our pheasants and chickens dashed aimlessly into the yard fences. Arizona Kid, one of our racing stallions, whinnied from a nearby pasture. He snorted and pawed the air, and then he lay down to roll violently, as though he were experiencing an acute pain. Little Tyke came bounding around one of the buildings, flinging her more than three hundred and fifty pounds of frightened weight directly at me. Margaret stood wide-eyed and screaming at the porch of our house, and I noticed for the first time that the buildings and chimneys were dancing and swaying crazily against the horizon. Across the river, toward the little village, I could see bricks tumbling, crashing on the roofs of the homes as they fell. Then I realized it was an earthquake.

It was not easy to struggle out from under this frightened and whimpering lioness as she clung to me for protection. I beckoned to Margaret to come away from the swaying buildings. In seconds it was over, but we devoted the next half hour to calming this huge creature who had flung herself into my arms for protection from the unknown. Then we made the rounds of the ranch, quietly talking to and stroking each of the animals in turn as they pushed their way up to the caressing hands of their mistress and master.

It was then that my mind wandered back to the days of my childhood, where, while sitting in my mother's lap, I had first heard these familiar words from the Bible, "And have dominion over the fish of the sea, and over the fowl of the air, and over every living thing that moveth upon the earth." Genesis 1:28. This sovereign authority has always been a challenge to me, in that this power, or right, of governing and controlling should also be used in assuring and consoling these creatures in time of distress. This experience was a demonstration of their confidence in our ability to comfort and allay their fears.

It was at this time, I think, that I fully realized that where there is no fear there is no savagery. The lioness had sought for me to allay her fears in a moment of paramount bewilderment. Some persons had predicted that during some such experience as this Little Tyke would go berserk and "revert to the wild." Surely when she had reached maturity and approached the mating season she would destroy anything in her way in her effort to find a mate. I wanted to ask these prognosticators some questions, but I smilingly turned aside. I

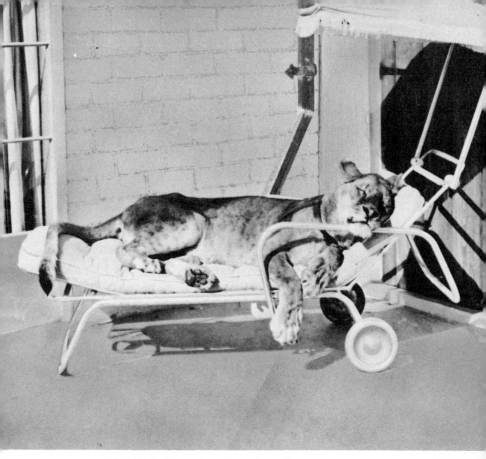

Little Tyke "lives it up" on the patio.

analyzed the fact that if I were to go to Africa, and a lion were to kill me, that would be termed "savagery;" but if I were to invade their faraway retreats and kill these regal creatures, that would be termed "sportsmanship." How biased can we become? If a cornered animal dare fight for its life, we chest-beating bipeds proclaim it "savage." By the same token, let us analyze ourselves. We spend more than 75 per cent of our time and energy in the fields of war, maiming and destroying our fellow man. Of the last 3,000 years of history there have been fewer than 225 spent in peace, away from the lust of man against man in his mad and ruthless killing. Indeed, we have become the most vicious beasts ever to roam this earth; and while wading waist deep in our brothers' blood, we have looked away from the truth about the animals of the jungle.

Have you ever looked deep into the soft brown eyes of a dying deer, with the blood streaming from its mouth and the gaping wound you made through its magnificent lungs? While standing there, have you ever wished to bring back the last precious moments of its life? No, I dare say you have not, for the lust of Nimrod overwhelmed you. And you ate with gusto the flesh of an animal whose only protection lay in its fleet hoofs—not fleet enough to outrun your bullet.

During your rare moments of shame, you came up with the alibi that these creatures (though they know no protecting savagery), if left, would become so numerous that they would be destructive to crops. This alibi has not stood under the overwhelming proof of the Kruger Park of South Africa, established in 1906 amid protests that animals would multiply and destroy farmers' crops and human lives.

According to my understanding of the Holy Bible, all animals were tame and more docile in the beginning. Then came Noah's great-grandson, Nimrod, who at that time was the most wicked ruler the world had ever seen. He was not content with the usual pleasures of life, but went forth to seek new thrills. He became a mighty hunter, killing animals, taking lives he could not replace. Animals became afraid and sought places to hide. If you don't think an animal has the same sense of feeling and hurt that you have, try pricking one slightly with a pin and see if he doesn't react as you do when you prick yourself. And so with our killings (call it "sportsman-ship" or whatever you like), we have helped create this great fear among animals. Then if they are cornered and dare to fight for their lives, we call them "savage."

Man was given dominion over all the animals of the earth. In the day of reckoning what will be our feeble alibi for what we have done to these beautiful creatures?

A news story carries this cruel indictment of so-called "human" beings: "The State Game Department, several years ago, had a couple of black bear cubs that were used as attractions at various county fairs as part of its exhibit. Naturally, the cubs kept growing, until when the fair circuit was over, the problem became what to do with them. None of the zoos were interested. They had all the bears they needed. So someone suggested they be turned loose in the Okanogan, where they had last been shown. 'Let the hunters get them!' was the general idea. So two days before hunting season, they were released. Now, those cubs had for several months known only that men fed them. After two days of little of what you'd call delectable food, one of them was spied by a hunter. Bawling like all get-out the cub came tearing down the side hill toward that hunter. He would have said, 'I'm hungry,' if he could. The excited hunter finally killed him, when he was but a few feet away. And when the hunter reached town with his trophy, the story he told of being attacked by that bear was printed far and wide. It has remained a well-kept secret up to now—but here goes the exposé!"

Where is man's sportsmanship, justice, decency, or fair play?

Pulling a Sled

✦✦✦

ONE crisp winter day, when a light blanket of new-fallen snow had transformed the valley into a glistening winter wonderland, I noticed a small neighbor boy coming down the trail with his sled flung over his shoulder. There was an obvious expression of disappointment in his young face as he slowly began to speak. "I hooked my dog, Pepper, to my sled to see if he would pull me; but instead, he turned around and snapped at me, and I was afraid." Then, as if he hardly dared continue, he asked, "Do you think Little Tyke would?"

This amused me, yet the serious look which shone in his eyes demanded a like answer. I pondered the question for a few moments. I knew the boy lacked confidence at every turn. At school he had been bullied by other boys of his class until, at last, his worried parents had sent him to a parochial school. I knew the lad suffered from feelings of inferiority, and I was anxious to do something for him.

"We'll try," I said with a laugh, then quickly added,

"if we can coax her away from the warm fireside and television!" I realized that here might be a step in the right direction toward solving his problem, giving him the confidence he needed. So I took the lad by the hand and led the way to the ranch house.

There I roused Little Tyke and put on her leash-harness. This was a truly new venture. At times of excitement Little Tyke had pulled my full weight along as she tugged at her leash, but would she stand to be hitched to a sled as a beast of burden? I picked up a nearby camera as we made our way out into the snow, where I commanded Little Tyke to halt while I tied two small ropes to the sides of her harness. I wound each around the sled's steering gear and gave the ends to the excited boy. "Pull tight, so they won't slip!" I yelled as I focused the camera on this strange scene. With a click I took the first picture and then pulled at the slide to change the film holder. When I looked up again I could scarcely believe my eyes. Little Tyke was laying into the harness with magnificent strides as though she enjoyed every minute of it, while the boy broke into loud laughter. I quickly took several more pictures, for this was another historical and unbelievable "first." Later that afternoon I developed the negatives in my darkroom and then made several large prints. I then called a friend of mine who worked for the newspaper, and I was proudly and pleasantly surprised the next day when I saw the fruits of my efforts displayed on the front page of a newspaper in the largest city in our state.

The following day the wires of the Associated Press picked it up and carried it to the far corners of the earth. The letters began pouring in, seeking verification of this unusual display. I was even more pleasantly surprised.

Also, many of these letters were addressed to the young lad, in my care. A group from the CBS television offices in New York telephoned me and asked if they might take some motion pictures of this unbelievable event. When they came with their equipment the light snow had melted, so we drove to the nearby mountains for their shots. I shall never forget the look in this young lad's eyes as he watched the results over coast-to-coast television. At the conclusion, the newscaster, Douglas Edwards, remarked, "You don't believe it? Well, neither did I, until I actually saw it!"

Beautifully written letters continued to come in huge numbers until the boy proudly displayed a large scrapbook full, including pictures from newspapers in all parts of the world. From then on he was called a celebrity and a hero. I smiled as I saw the real truth. Here was more than *one* miracle—it had also bolstered the confidence and faith of that youth.

Film of Little Tyke

❦❦❦

ALL through Little Tyke's life I had taken colored motion pictures of this marvelous animal and her remarkable adventures. These were intended only as our personal records to be enjoyed as the years went by. Occasionally we would show them to visiting friends, and I think once at a public gathering.

From then on the requests were overwhelming. They came from far and near, but we felt we could not afford to have duplicates made or bear the cost of applying sound tracks with music, narration, and sound effects to the film. Also, to run the original repeatedly would eventually ruin the film. Then, too, there was too much work here at the ranch; so we declined as politely as possible in each instance.

A young man, who was president of the social functions at his college in the eastern section of our state, telephoned me repeatedly and periodically for almost two years, until we finally relented and promised to show the silent film and present Little Tyke in person after the show. He was to furnish the public-address system with microphones, the music, an operator to run the projectors, and enough money to pay my expenses. He quickly promised to do all these things and we then agreed on a date.

At the college we sought out the president and made a survey of the stage entrance through which we would bring Little Tyke. The auditorium had a seating capacity of 2,500 and at the early hour of six-thirty the people began streaming in. Margaret came over to inquire what other attraction was to be shown here this night, and became speechless with surprise when she learned that Little Tyke and the film were the only ones.

Long before the starting time of eight o'clock the seats were filled to capacity; then the bannisters, the window sills, and the aisles were packed full. This was all new to Margaret, and to add to her perplexity, I hadn't prepared a single word for the narration. However, she sat in the car with Little Tyke and waited for the cue to bring her on to the stage and place her on a davenport where a spotlight would pick them up after the picture.

Explaining the pictures came easy, as I recalled the instances when I had taken them, and the soft music of the organ set them off impressively. During the scene where Little Tyke and the lamb ate and played together, I quoted the prophecy from the Bible. I was astonished when I peered from the projection room to see countless

The lioness and the lamb lie down together.

handkerchiefs wiping away tears from the eyes of many in the audience.

At the end of the picture, Margaret's cue was not necessary, for the applause was deafening. When the curtains parted and the spotlight shone on that scene on the davenport, it was with pride and satisfaction that I spoke to the vast audience.

I had just said, "Good night," when without warning the unexpected happened. Hundreds of children and grownups came clambering upon the stage. Canes and crutches were lost in the scramble as even small babes-in-arms were pushed forward to touch this great creature. I pleaded over the nearest microphone for fear that Little Tyke might playfully roll on some small baby. I pleaded again and again for a narrow passageway that we might escape through the eager crowd to our car.

After what seemed like hours we made our way to the stage door and quickly rushed into the darkness. But here more hundreds were gathered as we slowly elbowed our way to the car. As Little Tyke bounded into her car, a breathless boy rushed up to Margaret beside me and pantingly exclaimed, "I didn't think I'd get to touch her, but just as she leaped into the car I stuck out my hand and stroked her!" His beaming eyes danced with joy as he vanished into the darkness.

Within a few days we received a letter from the president of the college society which read in part, "It is almost beyond words to express our deep and sincere appreciation to you for appearing on our college campus last Saturday night with Little Tyke. . . . And as we sat entranced at the pictorial portrayal of the day-by-day growth of Little Tyke, the beauty of living as it is lived on Hidden Valley Ranch where fear is unknown and love is immeasurable, we were made homesick for heaven. We truly long for the day when men will lay down their guns; where fear and revenge will be no more; when they shall not hurt or destroy again; where the lion and lamb can lie down together and a little child shall lead them. The compliments are still coming in by the dozens every day expressing their sentiments and appreciation for such a remarkable and unbelievable program."

Some two months later another letter followed. "We are still receiving unnumbered reports of your splendid program of last October. Some of them have said it has been the best program presented here for the last forty years." As I read these last lines to Margaret I could hardly believe my eyes, but as I reached over and gave Little Tyke a gentle pat, I felt both proud and thankful that the silent film and Little Tyke's personal appearance had so bountifully pleased these wonderful people. I remembered, too, that before we had driven away from that college we had received telephone calls from distant cities and states asking us to appear. I don't know how the word of our appearance and the manner in which we were received had spread so fast.

Requests poured in from everywhere, it seemed. They wanted to see the film and the gentle lioness. After our appearance in Portland, Oregon, more letters of appreciation followed. Here are excerpts from a letter written by the man who engaged us: "I have attended many programs in Portland and other places, but must confess yours is different. While looking at the picture, 'The Life of Little Tyke,' the thoughts of the gloryland, where not only the lion and the lamb, but all the animals will lie down together, went through my mind. I am led to believe that God gave this unusual lioness to be an object lesson to help all who see her to change much of their thinking. It also seems quite providential that this animal should be placed in your home, for where in this wide world could one find another place where she would have met with the same understanding? The picture carried many thrills, but the thrill of the evening came when the curtain lifted on a living scene—your wife and Little Tyke together on the davenport. Think of it! A large lioness, with no cage, no leash, no anything, but being guided and controlled by the power of kindness and love."

There had been so many requests for pictures of Little Tyke and the lamb lying down together, that we had thousands printed to sell at a nominal cost. On several occasions we ran out of them, and it was on such an occasion that I suggested that those desiring a picture could write their names on a sheet of paper, and I would see to it that they received a picture, and they could send me the money after they received it.

Here again, I must take excerpts from one of the hundreds of letters which followed. "Your wonderful picture of Little Tyke and the lamb was received, and I'm sorry to have been so slow in sending the money. I had to wait for payday. I'm very proud of that picture. When I get a glass frame for it, Little Tyke shall share our living-room wall with just one other picture—He, too, has a lamb in His arms. It is one of Jesus. I'm twenty-eight," the writer continued, "but I'm not ashamed to say I cried that night you showed the picture at Meadow Glade. I wanted to put my arm around her so badly. Man has been so cruel to animals! I'm glad you've shown the world what tenderness will do. When the earth is made new again they will all live in peace. I hope someday we can visit your ranch and see her again."

Later we learned that a famous director connected with one of Hollywood's leading motion-picture studios took a two-year leave of absence in order that he and his writers might prepare a screen story for Little Tyke, which he hoped to produce.

Imp

HE approach to Hidden Valley Ranch from the east
is by way of a long, winding road down the hillside.
It was while driving down this hill late one night
that I noticed a small, dark object disappear into the
ditch at the roadside. It slipped along too slowly for
some wild thing, so I stopped, and with my flashlight in
hand I searched the wet grass. I heard a weak, plaintive
mewing, and spied a small black kitten huddled, drip-
ping wet, in the cold, rainy night. He had apparently
been tossed thoughtlessly into the wilderness from a
passing car. I quickly slipped him into the pocket of my
warm jacket and continued on toward the ranch house.
I approached the glowing fireplace where Margaret sat
reading, and quietly slipped the kitten into her lap. I
knew we already had too many cats, so I hastened to
explain that early the next morning I would see if one of
our neighbors would take him. If they didn't, I would
painlessly put him to sleep; but I knew full well Margaret would fight for his life.

Imp makes himself at home.

Quickly she gathered the already purring little creature up in her cupped hands and made for the kitchen, where she warmed some milk. The little fellow had not been weaned, for it scarcely knew how to lap. The following morning, when the sun had dried the dew, I placed the soft black kitten on the lawn for his sunbath. Curious peacocks were the first to discover him, screaming their wild, raucous warnings, as they did when a strange animal approached. The frightened kitten rolled backward, then stiffened into a tiny black mite as his eyes grew wide and his tail grew bushy. Like a bullet, he catapulted into a retreat for safety. In the distance he hesitated momentarily, to stare at Little Tyke, who was watching all the while. We watched this fast-shifting scene, when, with a swift dash, the kitten flung himself between the huge, sprawling paws of the lioness. Here, while her noble head towered above him, the tiny mite settled down in contentment. The peafowl sputtered and clucked momentarily, but soon settled to their routine of the day. We knew then we would never give him away. After a quick sniff Little Tyke realized that this was not Pinky, but her motherly instincts were apparent as she nuzzled and licked this little creature.

When the kitten grew older he became sprightly and mischievous. He teased and tormented the other cats, then retreated to the bosom of his huge protector. When he became hungry he demanded his food with a loud mew and a scratch. If unnoticed, he leaped squarely upon his mistress and continued to beg for his food. We searched endlessly for a suitable name, until one day we decided it should be "Imp."

Imp became very fond of Little Tyke as the months went by, and she returned that love with enough patience to overlook his mischievous tricks. He soon learned to attract our attention by scratching his sharp claws on the glass of the French door leading in from our patio; then as we turned the knob, he would pop in like a pinched pumpkin seed, where his first duty was to sniff all four of Little Tyke's footpads, and then her nose. Next he would curl up snugly against her for a nap. These scientists who steadfastly claim that a house cat and a lion will not fraternize should have been there to witness some of their antics.

Little Tyke, plodding down the wooded trails, following closely behind her mistress, was a usual sight to the visitor, but a careful eye could also see a black kitten walking daintily between the lioness's two front feet. When Little Tyke raised to stretch her full length and to sharpen her claws on the bark of a tree, little Imp seemed dwarfed as he aped her from below. Aside from Pinky, Imp was the only cat with which Little Tyke would share her food.

A Host of Friends

❤❤❤

FOR some reason Little Tyke inspired men and women in every part of the world and from every walk
of life to write thousands of beautiful letters and
cards, also to write poetry about her. She inspired some
to create beautiful images of her on canvas.

One woman at first said she was going to be afraid to
get out of her car when she arrived at Hidden Valley
Ranch, but she melted under the awe-inspiring gentleness of the noble creature who came up to nuzzle her.
Later she wrote the following poem to Little Tyke:

Lovely, tawny Little Tyke,
With gorgeous jungle eyes
Lit with innocence of youth,
And yet with wisdom, wise;
How can I ever thank you
For the lovely time with you;
A thrill I never will forget
When first you came in view?
I still can feel your gentle kiss
Upon my hand and arm;

Your jaws wide open, baring teeth
With ne'er a thought of harm.
Your furred and lovely massive head,
Your eyes, and silky ears—
I could sit beside you there
With neither qualms nor fears.
Oh, tame and lovely jungle beast,
We are so far apart,
And yet, for one brief afternoon
Our lives touched, heart to heart.

(89)

Little Tyke and Margaret at Hidden Valley Ranch.

What was there about Little Tyke that caused people to react so strangely? For instance, when we were stopping at the beach in California with my sister, prior to making a television appearance, we frequently walked Little Tyke along the beach after midnight, so we might attract as little attention as possible. She loved to run and bat at the waves with those huge, gentle paws. On the return, she always walked atop the four-foot sea wall beside the plank walk.

It was on our return from one of these walks that we noticed a young couple sitting in a car in the moonlight watching the restless sea. When we approached, the young man sprang from his car directly for us. Little Tyke stopped to watch him. He didn't hesitate for a second, but leaned confidently against the wooden sea wall and thrust both his arms around her as he exclaimed in a delighted undertone, "Isn't she a beautiful lioness!" I inquired if he was accustomed to rushing up to lions and hugging them in this fashion. He admitted that he had never been this close to one before, nor had he ever touched one, but somehow, when he saw her he immediately realized his lack of fear, and that in place of fear there was a sudden love for this huge creature.

Taking Motion Pictures

✴✴✴

T HEN came the time when we were to appear on a coast-to-coast television program. Television's split-second timing made it necessary to film parts of the scenes. This was done "on location" in beautiful Beverly Hills, California. When Art Baker, the master of ceremonies, appeared and before he had seen Little Tyke, I heard him say to one of the cameramen, "I hear I am to work with a tame African lioness today, which reminds me of a story I heard before I left the studio. There was an old man sitting in church one Sabbath day, listening to the minister preaching about the lion lying down with the lamb. When the preacher had concluded, the inquiring man stood up and directing his words to the pastor, said, 'It says in the Bible that the lion shall lie down with the lamb, but, Mr. Pastor, does it say anywhere in the Bible which one shall get up alone?' "

Well, that was Art's conception of a gentle lioness— until he saw Little Tyke! During the first scene, where Little Tyke and Margaret went to the door to meet Art,

I stood on the sidelines waiting. I knew the first few seconds would be the all-important ones. What kind of person was this Art Baker, and would Little Tyke like him? I didn't have long to wait. As Art stood waiting for a response to his knock at the door, Little Tyke nosed her way out to greet him as Margaret opened the door. Without a second's hesitation, Art leaned down to pat her friendly head and shake her outstretched paw. At the end of the first filmed scene I heard him exclaim to one of the cameramen, "This is wonderful. It's fantastic!"

The next scene was to be taken with some chickens. I felt at ease because at home on the ranch the lioness roamed among them every day; but when the chickens' were brought in, I stood with wide eyes. The chickens were four little day-old chicks. My thoughts sped quickly back to Little Tyke's only experience with day-old chicks at Hidden Valley Ranch! A hen and her chicks had wandered on to the lawns surrounding our home and I had thought nothing of it until later, when I noticed Little Tyke acting peculiarly, with a guilty look and lips held tightly closed over obviously open jaws, she stealthily slunk by the house. I called sharply, "Tyke! What have you got?" Instantly her mouth flew open, and out popped one of the little chicks I had seen only moments before hopping across the lawns. I could hardly believe my eyes as the little chick, unharmed, flapped his down-covered wings and almost flew back to his sputtering mother. Little Tyke had apparently been

Day-old chicks, safe in the lion's mouth!

licking the tiny chick when with one "slurp" of that huge tongue, the little chick had popped right into her mouth, and with perplexed, motherly dignity, she hadn't known just how to fondle it further.

This now was to be her second contact with these tiny creatures, and more amazed was I when we got our instructions for the scene with Little Tyke and the chicks. These were the instructions: The four tiny chicks were to be placed on the grass before the huge cameras, which were manipulated from rails resembling railroad tracks. "Little Tyke is to come into camera view, walk over to the chicks, hesitate over them for about fifteen seconds, and then walk off the scene." With further amazement I retorted, "This isn't Clark Gable. It's an African lioness, who has seen little chicks only once before in her whole life!"

Came the sharp counter-question, "Can't she do it?"

This was a challenge to our dignity, and I commanded her gently, "Tyke, you heard the man." To the astonishment of everyone, myself most of all, as the cameras ground away Little Tyke strode gracefully into camera view and hesitated over the tiny nestled chicks long enough to lick them very gently with but the tip of her tongue, then, with a yawn, as though the whole thing bored her, she strode from camera view. Later she came back to lie down with the chicks. They immediately made their way into Little Tyke's long silky hair at the base of her neck. Two of them peered out from the shelter of their new protector while we watched in amazement.

Next came the scene with the kitten. Someone brought in a tiny gray Persian kitten and handed it to me with these instructions: "Little Tyke is to lie in the foreground of the camera's range and the kitten is to walk into view and over to Tyke, walk over her legs, curl up and go to sleep between her paws." I couldn't believe my ears! Nevertheless, in a sort of dumb stupor, I patted the kitten a few times until the crew was ready; then I stooped over and placed the tiny creature on the grass and gave it a similar command, which I didn't even dare

A little child shall drive them!

dream it would follow. I wanted to throw up my hands and quit, but as I turned with perplexed emotion, I saw this tiny creature, with its tail straight in the air, daintily lifting its feet high and putting them down again, going directly to where Little Tyke was lying. There the kitten smelled each of Little Tyke's four paws, crawled over her outstretched foreleg, sat down and gazed from side to side at those huge jaws above its head as if to say, "Now I'm safe!" Little Tyke's dignity and motherly love had conquered all fear, and everyone stood there in awe. Little Tyke crooked one paw as if to hold the tiny creature closer to her breast.

The next scene was to be with a lamb. An agricultural college had graciously furnished two. However, when we placed them before Little Tyke, in order that she might make her own choice, she sniffed each one lightly and walked away, wrinkling her nose in distaste. The lambs had been carefully bathed, according to our instructions, as we knew Little Tyke disliked objectionable odors; but to her keen nose, there was still something offensive about those sniffs. Besides, the lambs were only a few weeks old and were bleating constantly because they had been taken from their mothers. This created quite a problem. Little Tyke didn't like the odors, and the lambs wanted their mothers. They were hungry. We tried to make them nurse from a bottle, but this was new to them. The cow's milk didn't taste right, and, well, they just wouldn't nurse. Margaret came up with a wonderful idea. "Little Tyke loves perfume," she said with a laugh as she handed me a bottle of cologne. I rubbed the contents vigorously into the soft wool of one of the lambs and placed it near Little Tyke. This did the trick splendidly, while the cameramen had a field day.

The next shot was to be of Little Tyke pulling the producer's seven-year-old daughter in a little wagon. Now, this would not have been difficult at all had it not been for the fact that this little girl's older brother had been diligently "coaching" his baby sister for several weeks. (Ever since he had known she was to be the little girl in the act.) The "coaching," I learned, had been along these lines: "Just you wait until that lion gets you in the wagon! She'll turn around, and with one gulp, you'll be gone!"

Our first problem then, was to acquaint the little girl with the lamb, and to have her hold and stroke it. After her fear of the lamb had vanished I called to Little Tyke and she came over to lick the lamb some more. Fear in the little girl was soon replaced with confidence and love, as the lioness, the girl, and the lamb played daintily on the lawns. I went to the child's wagon and saw that no preparation had been made for hitching Little Tyke to it. I could use Little Tyke's harness-leash on her, but how would I hitch her to the wagon? I looked around and found two weak and spindly sticks. I then tied one end of each of these sticks to the front axle of the wagon and the other ends to Little Tyke's harness-leash while the huge cameras and their tracks were being laboriously moved to new positions.

I marveled at this African lioness standing so patiently in one position while we worked feverishly. I knew, also, that we were working against time. We were allotted two days "shooting" time, not to exceed three! I made the final preparations by utilizing a long leash for the reins, and lifted the little girl into the wagon for a few last-moment instructions. Then we waited. The camera crew were not ready, and Little Tyke had to stand in that one position in the hot California sun for what seemed hours, her misery aggravated by a debilitating cold from which she was suffering. If she were to lie down, the makeshift shafts would splinter and break.

The time finally came when the camera crew said they were ready, but here was another serious problem. The direction in which (for camera-track reasons) Little Tyke had to pull the little girl was slightly downhill and on a paved driveway. We had no hold-back straps on the harness, and I knew the wagon would bump Little Tyke's heels at every step. But we tried, and everything went smoothly, except for one thing—the camera men had forgotten to put in the wide-angle lens. They had been too close to get the whole picture without "panning" back and forth from Little Tyke to the girl, which was not good. The word "retake" was not welcomed by us any more than by poor Little Tyke. However, we waited some more until the camera crew changed the lens and readied themselves. This time Little Tyke seemed to lack her usual enthusiasm, but she plodded on until a huge dog appeared out of nowhere, snapping and snarling close to Little Tyke's heels. She whirled to protect herself, and as she did, both shafts broke into splinters.

The little girl sat through this as calmly as though it was only routine; however, Little Tyke began showing signs of fatigue. In between shots she wandered about, smelling the beautiful flowers or just lying in the shade. The sun was terribly hot, and she was accustomed to the cooler climate of the State of Washington. We tried to give her some rest periods, but a big cat doesn't really rest and regain spent strength in short "cat-nap" periods. Lions or other members of the feline family are very different from the canine, or dog, family. Cats lie around and sleep a lot, while dogs can trot all day. When we felt Little Tyke's nose and footpads becoming abnormally warm, we begged to be excused for the day. Our attention was immediately called to the fact that cameras and camera crews on location cost a lot of money, so we continued. We finished all the film "shooting" in eight hours—a feat which I later learned was originally scheduled to take two or three days. During the last scene Little Tyke didn't respond as she usually did, and I knew she was ill.

We retired to my sister's home at the beach again, and it was during that night that her running nose showed proof of her illness. During the next weeks we pampered her as much as possible. In two weeks we were to appear on a live national television show, supported by the film we had already completed. During the interim, thousands had learned of her whereabouts and begged to see her. Others didn't ask; they just climbed the wooden fence. Consequently Little Tyke did not get a chance to recuperate as we had hoped.

Came the day for the show, and we were notified to appear six hours before the telecast in order to rehearse several times if necessary. The southern midsummer heat was terrific, and the stage lights were hotter. In between rehearsals we tried to find a shady spot on the studio lot for Little Tyke to rest; but wherever we went, there were the crowds of admirers and the curious people.

When the time came for the real show, Little Tyke

was too warm to take her place on the stage. We were the last feature to appear, so the producers gave us permission to wait off stage where the temperature was a few degrees cooler. As I look back now, I marvel at the confidence Little Tyke had instilled in that crew during her three-week stay in Hollywood. They knew that if anyone "goofed," or if Little Tyke refused to go on stage at the proper moment, the split-second timing under which a live show is telecast would be thrown out of balance, and the national hook-up made at tremendous expense would be a failure.

As Margaret, Little Tyke, and I stood off stage waiting for our cue, I could hear my heart thump as little fears crept into my mind. They need not have, however, for on the designated second Little Tyke walked confidently between her mistress and me, past huge, moving cameras, under shifting booms and over wriggling cables which were swinging to our set. There she took her place between Margaret and me on a davenport. She tried to tell her mistress that she wasn't well, and that she wanted to rest; but there wasn't room, and it was much too hot. Under all these trying conditions, she carried on like the trouper she was.

At the opening of the show, Art Baker picked up a Bible and read these impressive words: "The wolf and the lamb shall feed together, and the lion shall eat straw like the bullock." Isaiah 65:25.

Little Tyke performed magnificently during the entire show, and at the conclusion the executive producer

8—L.T.

came over to me and asked if I would permit the audience, who were watching a monitor in an adjoining studio, to come in and view this spectacle. We remained in our last position until all of the producers, crewmen, and entire audience had shaken our hands. Apparently they needed reassurance that Little Tyke was real.

Knowing that Little Tyke's health was at stake, immediately after the show which was followed by a tremendous wave of congratulations, we got into Little Tyke's own car, with her name in chrome-covered bronze lettering on each side, and drove directly for Washington, twelve hundred miles away, where we knew Little Tyke could rest. I drove steadily for twenty-six hours, stopping only long enough for food and gasoline, until with a weary, grateful sigh, we entered the portals of Hidden Valley Ranch.

At home, Little Tyke seemed to grow stronger and she ate heartily. However, there was a slight drainage from her nose. This we watched and treated. It was strange to see this huge African lioness walk up to Margaret like a little child and make herself understood that she wanted the mucus removed from her nose. She knew Margaret always carried a ready cleaning tissue.

We received many invitations to show the film, "The Life of Little Tyke," and to present Little Tyke in person, but because we wanted Little Tyke to have complete rest, we declined them all. Wandering about Hidden Valley Ranch or just sleeping in the sun had hitherto been as a tonic to this unusual creature, but now she responded slowly. During the trip and the first two weeks at home, she lost considerable weight, but she gained back most of it during the next three weeks. She had learned to sound the horn of her car when she wanted to go for a ride. This was accomplished by pressing her jaws against the steering wheel. After each blast of the horn she would look coyly about and roar to her heart's content. To avoid fatigue the trips were short, however.

From the studio in Hollywood, we learned that the response to Little Tyke's television appearance was so great it left no doubt in their minds but that she would win the highest award for the entire year. A few of the letters addressed to the studio were forwarded to us here at the ranch. One letter to Art Baker from Yonkers, New York, stands out in my memory. It read in part:

"DEAR ART: Nothing has made me happier than your picture of the lion and the lamb. It has helped me believe in the Bible. The owners should take her before the Big Four; it could be the means of a peace movement."

I marveled many times at the ability of the producers and directors of the television show. How they were able to view the films which I had taken of Little Tyke during her life and were able to touch on the most important high lights in those few fleeting moments of television!

One evening in July, after a playful day, Little Tyke reluctantly left the fireside and television to retire to her room at nine-thirty o'clock. The next morning, when I went to awaken her, I was frightened when I heard her groaning with pain. She was unable to stand or to get out of bed. I called to Margaret to summon the veterinarians. Then I turned and saw that Little Tyke had somehow managed to get to her feet momentarily, and had followed me out onto the lawns, where she fell. I truly believe Little Tyke knew that the end was near and wanted her benefactor, whom she trusted so implicitly, to hold her close in the last precious moments of her life.

She died peacefully and quickly in my arms here at Hidden Valley Ranch, while I sat on the lawns she loved so well, stroking her magnificent head. The pupils of her soft eyes dilated, then grew small as I listened to those soft and anxious whimpers which only Margaret and I understood. I heard the veterinarian's car speeding up our driveway as Little Tyke sighed lightly and slumped to sleep.

She succumbed to virus pneumonia, an ailment which she had not been able to conquer since she contracted the disease only a few weeks previously, while working so hard, yet so willingly, in Hollywood. The sudden change in climate had been too much for her.

"Lion of My Dreams"

❧❧ ❧❧ ❧❧

L ITTLE TYKE'S life is over. She had to pass this last hurdle in order to prove to some of the skeptical and more fearful human creatures that she would not someday turn on the hands that fed her or perhaps someone else.

Of the many who came to see Little Tyke in the days before she died, two were missionaries who had spent many years in Africa. They were amazed at their lack of fear as she bravely endeavored to frolic with them on the lawn. That night, as they preached in their church, they quoted these words from the Bible: "Perfect love casteth out fear," to express the magnitude of the enlightening truth they had just learned. How true! And to those wondrous words I will add our philosophy, "Where there is no fear there can be no savagery." Little Tyke reflected the love and care which Margaret and I had given her, just as all human beings can receive only the reflection of love as it has been unselfishly given.

We feel some measure of consolation in reminding

ourselves of the rare privilege we enjoyed in our close association with this noble creature and the love she had poured out to us from her great heart.

Little Tyke's sudden and untimely death was like a shocking thunderbolt from a clear sky. The thousands of beautifully written letters and cards of sympathy we have received give us a comforting warmth. It has been many months since Little Tyke died, but still the letters pour in, some carrying newspaper and magazine clippings from all parts of this great country and some foreign lands.

I think of an eminent attorney in whose office hangs a large picture of Little Tyke and the lamb as a symbol of complete accord. Here, when confronted with those who seek the divorce court, he smilingly points to this picture of the two with such diverse natures lying happily, enjoying each other's love. He happily relates that this object lesson has been successful on some occasions.

Of the thousands of letters and cards of sympathy, I think the following is one which remains foremost in our fond memories: "In going through old letters in my desk not long ago, I found this letter to Little Tyke. It was written in 1947 or '48 and never sent. After all, she had so many friends! I felt perhaps the best way to thank you was not to add the burden of another letter. Perhaps that still holds true, now more than ever. Yet it expressed what I feel is a universal thought which many others shared, and still share with you: 'Where there is no fear there is peace and trust, and friendliness,' even in the animal kingdom. Little Tyke has gone away, and many people are deeply and sincerely sorry, but her warmth and great gentleness will continue to live for those to whom she was more than a lion—in some ways more than a 'human'—a nature ruled by trust and love. Thank you for letting me meet her personally. I loved her very much, and still do."

Here are the contents of the letter she enclosed, the letter which had been written more than seven years before: "DEAR LITTLE TYKE: Once many years ago, more than fifty in fact, a little girl sat on the floor of an old brown house in Ohio talking to a picture she held in her hand. The picture was of a lion's head, and was a trademark cut from a coffee package. As a very great privilege the little girl had been allowed to play with it, for her mother was saving those coupons in a cigar box until enough was collected to 'send in' and get the little girl 'something for Christmas.' But nothing in the book of premiums was as thrilling, from the child's standpoint, as this moment and the joy of 'getting to hold' the shaggy head in her hand and gaze into the strange, whimsical, friendly eyes! She talked aloud to the picture just as she did to her dog, the beloved cats, and 'Old Girl,' the friendly hen. 'I love you,' she said. 'Someday I'm going to pet you, the *real live* you. Someday I will—.'

"The little girl, her mother and grandmother, moved far from that Ohio home in 1902, when she was ten, to become pioneer homesteaders in a new, wild, wide

Rest after a romp.

Paula Bane with Margaret and Tyke.

No fear of wolves in this company!

What a big kitty!

Art Baker entertains the Westbeaus and Little Tyke.

Conversation by the wayside.

Allen Young, with guest in Hollywood.

Pause in a seaside stroll.

Breakfast together at eight.

With Cecil B. de Mille in his studio.

Judge Homer T. Bone of the U.S. Circuit Court.

Playmates by the river at Hidden Valley Ranch.

prairieland. But the dream never quite left, and was carried with the child into womanhood. In fact it became a standard slogan for 'kidding' among family and friends, 'Oh, that she *would* pet a lion, if she had a chance!' And mentally, the girl, and the woman, always answered, 'Someday I *shall!* Someday I'm going to pet a lion—a real one!'

"Thank you, Little Tyke, for fulfilling the dream of a lifetime—an old lady's dream that persisted fifty years and more. Thank you for being Little Tyke, and thanks, so many thanks to your good people for understanding and knowing how to bring you up to trust people who love animals. Someday you will be famous and have a story written about you.

"If I were younger, and had the good eyesight and inspirational writing ability of younger years, I would like to write a story about you for children as a labor of love. But now I want to tell you there never was a more complete fulfillment of a dream than feeling your warm tongue around my hand or holding all seventy-five pounds of you for a picture. It has been many years since I lifted seventy-five pounds, but I'm mighty proud of the evidence of the fulfillment of that lifelong wish.

"And there's another dream in my heart, Little Tyke —not as old, perhaps, but even more deeply sincere! The dream that the lion will one day lie down with the lamb in the hearts of men as you have proved to be true in the animal world—where there is no fear. All that is needed is for men, races and nations, to know one another, and to trust and understand one another as you trust your people and as they have understood you!

"Thank you again, Little Tyke, for being, even for a brief moment, 'the lion of my childhood dreams.' "

Recently Art Baker wrote a letter to a popular magazine, eulogizing Little Tyke. We quote his letter as it appeared in the "Letters to the Editor column" of that magazine:

"In 'The Sad Story of the Gentle Lion' your 'Little Tyke' pictures were a wonderful tribute to an extraordinary animal. She spent three weeks with us in Hollywood prior to her appearance on 'You Asked for It,' her television debut, and, unfortunately, her only national live appearance. Public response to her television appearance shows that she was one of the best-liked performers to appear on the program in 1955. Signed, Art Baker, Hollywood, California."

Every few days we still receive letters from the Seattle Children's Orthopedic Hospital acknowledging the receipt of money which has been donated in the memory of Little Tyke—money which will help other little tykes to get well and to become strong, healthy men and women.

Little Tyke is now a legend, a loving care we shall never be able to forget.